Embraced *by* God

Seven Promises for Every Woman

A Bible Study by
BABBIE MASON

ABINGDON PRESS
Nashville

Scripture quotations marked CEB are from the Common English Bible. Copyright © 2011 by the Common English Bible. All rights reserved. Used by permission. www.CommonEnglishBible.com.

Scripture quotations marked *King James 2000* are taken from the King James 2000e © 2011 Robert A. and Thelma J. Couric.

Scripture quotations marked KJV are from The Authorized (King James) Version. Rights in the Authorized Version in the United Kingdom are vested in the Crown. Reproduced by permission of the Crown's patentee, Cambridge University Press.

Scripture quotations marked *THE MESSAGE* are from *THE MESSAGE*. Copyright © by Eugene H. Peterson 1993, 1994, 1995, 1996, 2000, 2001, 2002. Used by permission of NavPress Publishing Group.

Scripture quotations marked NCV are taken from the New Century Version®. Copyright © 2005 by Thomas Nelson, Inc. Used by permission. All rights reserved.

Scripture quotations marked NIV are taken from the Holy Bible, New International Version®, NIV®. Copyright © 1973, 1978, 1984, 2011 by Biblica, Inc.™ Used by permission of Zondervan. All rights reserved worldwide. www.zondervan.com. The "NIV" and "New International Version" are trademarks registered in the United States Patent and Trademark Office by Biblica, Inc.™

Scripture quotations marked NKJV are taken from the New King James Version®. Copyright © 1982 by Thomas Nelson, Inc. Used by permission. All rights reserved.

Scripture quotations marked NLT are taken from the *Holy Bible,* New Living Translation, copyright © 1996, 2004, 2007. Used by permission of Tyndale House Publishers, Inc., Carol Stream, Illinois 60188. All rights reserved.

Scripture quotations marked NRSV are taken from the New Revised Standard Version of the Bible, copyright 1989, Division of Christian Education of the National Council of the Churches of Christ in the United States of America. Used by permission. All rights reserved.

Babbie Mason, "You Are Not Alone" © 2011 Praise & Worship Works/ASCAP. Admin. by BMG Rights Management (US) LLC. All rights reserved. Used by permission.

Babbie Mason, "Each One, Reach One" © 1990 Praise & Worship Works/ASCAP. Admin. by BMG Rights Management (US) LLC. All rights reserved. Used by permission.

Babbie Mason, "I Love You, I Do" © 2009. Praise & Worship Works/ASCAP. Admin by BMG Rights Management (US) LLC. All rights reserved. Used by permission.

12 13 14 15 16 17 18 19 20 21—10 9 8 7 6 5 4 3 2 1

MANUFACTURED IN THE UNITED STATES OF AMERICA

CONTENTS

INTRODUCTION

Have you ever wondered, *Does God really love me? Does He accept me as I am? Do I really matter to Him?* If so, then rest assured that each and every question you have is of great concern to God. If you need reassurance of God's love for you or you long for a deeper, more personal and intimate relationship with Him, you've come to the right study!

This study is designed to help you understand with greater clarity God's deep, sweet love for you, and to experience this love as never before. The message is that God not only loves you . . . *you are His favorite!* He loves you as if you were the only one to love.

Just a couple of years ago my own eyes were opened to this profoundly new and life-changing understanding of God's love. It began one Sunday when my good friend Dr. Tony Ashmore, pastor of the Life Gate Church in Villa Rica, Georgia, instructed each person in the congregation to turn to one's neighbor and say, "I am God's favorite." Now, I was raised in church, a preacher's daughter turned Christian singer, songwriter, and recording artist. I've always known deep down that God loves me—and that was enough for me. But the idea that I could ever be God's favorite seemed to be overstepping a boundary. The thought seemed even a bit presumptuous. This motivated me to seek the truth of His Word, and what I discovered is . . . *it's absolutely true!*

Jesus said, "I will be in them and you will be in me so that they will be completely one. then the world will know that you sent me and that you loved them just *as much as you loved me.*" (John 17:23 NCV, emphasis added). As I pondered this verse and other passages in John 17, God quickened my heart, and I realized that God truly loves me just as much as He loves His own Son, Jesus! I also became deeply aware that everything

God gave to Jesus, He also has given to me. I am a rightful heir as a daughter of the Most High King! This awareness has taken my love relationship with Him to another level. *The realization of these promises has made me more keenly aware of God's loving presence and purpose in my life.*

I concluded that if I, a Christian for nearly fifty years, could come to a profoundly new understanding of God's love, then maybe you could, too! Seeing the need to encourage the hearts of women, I set out on a mission to share this life-changing message through the written word and through music. As a result, I have written a twenty-one day, life-affirming devotional, *Embraced by God*. I also have the great privilege to lead women into worship at conferences and retreats by sharing a special concert event called Embrace: A Worship Celebration for Women. At this event, I am blessed to share new songs that I've written. These songs of worship and encouragement are featured on the music CD *Embrace*. And now for groups there is this study: *Embraced By God: Seven Promises For Every Woman*.

In the next eight weeks, you and a group of friends will be embraced by God's love as you explore seven promises He makes to us as His beloved daughters. Each of these promises addresses a specific area in our love relationship with the Lord:

1. You Are Loved Unconditionally by God
2. You Are Beautiful to God
3. You Are Never Alone
4. You Have Everything You Need in God
5. You Have a God-given Purpose
6. You Can Accomplish Great Things in God's Name
7. You Are Equipped With Unique Gifts and Talents

Then, with the power of Jesus Christ operating within us, we can apply these beautiful aspects of His love to our lives.

Each week you will study and reflect on one specific promise, with a final week pulling it all together and sending you onward with the challenge to live *loved*.

There are five devotional readings for each of the eight weeks. Each reading begins with a Scripture verse and features the following segments:

Think About His Love	A devotional reflection that helps you to meditate on the promise and consider how it relates to your life.
Read About His Love	A guided study of Scripture with space for recording your responses.
Pray About His Love	Prayer suggestions with a sample prayer to guide you into your own conversation with God.
Be About His Love	Questions and activities to help you put your love walk into practice.

These readings can be completed in about 20-30 minutes. You will need a pen or pencil and your Bible. Another helpful tool you may want to have on hand is an inexpensive notebook or journal. A journal can be a place to write longer reflections, record prayers and answers to prayers, and journal about your *Embraced by God* journey. For your convenience, you will find some journaling pages at the back of this book.

During this study you also will be working on memorizing John 17:23, so that you can hide this profound truth deep in your heart and live with the joy of knowing you are loved relentlessly and without exception or condition. I especially like the New Century Version of this verse (see page 9). But if your group prefers another translation, you may choose to memorize the verse in that translation of the Bible.

Once a week you will gather with the other ladies in your group to watch a video guided by me. I encourage you to discuss what you're learning, and to share how the truths of God's Word are changing your own life. You will find that this experience will help you to grow in your ability to receive and give God's love, dramatically impacting every area of your life.

Before you begin this journey, give God permission to transform your thinking and change any myths and misconceptions you have about Him, or yourself. You will learn many new things about your loving heavenly Father, and you may even make some surprisingly new discoveries about who you are. When the study is complete, you will understand with more clarity *who you are in God and who He is in you.*

There is absolutely nothing more important than developing an intimate, life-changing relationship with the God who made you, loves you deeply, and knows you better than anyone else. Remember that, regardless of what is going on in your life or in the world around you, God's loving presence in your life will make all the difference in how you face each circumstance. You are deeply loved, tremendously blessed, and highly favored. Yes, you are His favorite. So, get ready to be embraced by God!

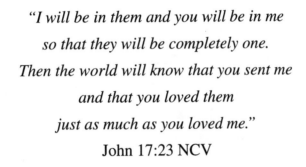

"I will be in them and you will be in me
so that they will be completely one.
Then the world will know that you sent me
and that you loved them
just as much as you loved me."
John 17:23 NCV

Week 1

YOU ARE LOVED UNCONDITIONALLY BY GOD

Imagine the most wonderful love relationship you could ever experience on earth. Envision a love without limits or conditions. Consider a relationship that is completely satisfying in every way; *now* visualize the height of this relationship and multiply that as high as you can count. If you could count all the way to infinity and beyond, your answer would still be far too small compared to how much God really loves you. His love for you is passionate, unconditional and far, far, beyond any love you could ever experience with another human being. Not only does the God of the universe love you; He wants more than anything for you to surrender every area of your life to Him and love Him in return.

This week you will read more about this unconditional, passionate love of God. As you go about your daily life this week, meditate on this promise: *God loves me just as much as He loves His Son, Jesus, and wants more than anything for me to love Him in return.*

Scripture Memorization

During the next eight weeks you will be working on memorizing John 17:23 (NCV), the core verse for this study:

"I will be in them and you will be in me so that they will be completely one. Then the world will know that you sent me and that you loved them just as much as you loved me."

Write the verse on several index cards and place them in handy and highly visible areas, such as your bathroom mirror, refrigerator, car dashboard, and bedside table. Read the verse when you get up, throughout the day, and as you go to bed. Another great way to memorize Scripture is to write or type it. Take a look at scripturetyper.com and give it a try!

DAY 1: YOU ARE GOD'S FAVORITE

"…you have loved them just as you loved me."
John 17:23 CEB

Think About His Love

When I was eight years old I accepted Christ and I am celebrating what I call my "Year of Jubilee," fifty years of knowing Christ as my Lord and Savior. Yet just a few years ago my eyes were opened to a new awareness of God's love. I was sitting in worship as the pastor told the congregation to turn to their neighbor and say the words, "I am God's favorite." Initially I thought, *How could I be God's favorite? I have a past filled with mistakes. I have issues and challenges in my life. There are so many people who must stand ahead of me in line for that prize.*

I have always known that God loves me, and I was satisfied with that. But to consider that I could ever be God's favorite? That seemed like overstepping a boundary, maybe even a little presumptuous or arrogant. But, I could not get that thought out of my mind, so I turned to the Scriptures for wisdom. It is certainly true that the Bible is the only book you can read and never finish, for each time you read the pages of the Word of God, you will receive new and fresh wisdom and insight for daily living.

I have discovered that we are all God's favorite. Each and every one of us is deeply loved by God—including you! Please understand that God does not prefer some of His children over others. God sees each of His children and loves them completely and shows them His great, compassionate favor. We are God's favored ones—not because of who we are or how good we may be or because of what we have accomplished in life. Even on our best day, we are still at our worst. The Bible says, "We are all as an unclean thing, and all our righteousnesses are as filthy rags; and we all do fade as a leaf; and our iniquities, like the wind, have taken us away" (Isaiah 64:6 KJV). You are God's favorite, not because of anything you have done, but because of what Jesus Christ did for you on the cross at Calvary. In your own strength you could never qualify to be God's favorite, but Jesus does. And because of Christ's great work at the cross, once and for all, He qualified you! This may be an amazing thought to grasp, but believe this truth and let it sink into your mind and down into your heart until it changes not only how you think but also how you live.

Be comforted and encouraged by the fact that Jesus prays for you. Several times in John 17, Jesus prays for those the Father has given Him and for those who would believe in Him through their message. Has it ever occurred to you that God has given you to Jesus? You, dear friend, are a gift from God to Jesus. You are not a burden, a liability, an irritation, an agitation, or an aggravation to Jesus. You are a gift from your Heavenly Father to His Son, and you bring His heart great joy. His thoughts are always turned toward you. Psalm 139:17-18 (NIV) says, "How precious to me are your thoughts, O God! How vast is the sum of them! Were I to count them, they would outnumber the grains of sand. When I awake, I am still with you." God's thoughts toward you far outnumber every grain of sand along the shores of every ocean, sea, river, lake, stream, and waterway combined!

You are of endless worth and value to God. Deuteronomy 7:6 (NLT) says, "You are a holy people, who belong to the Lord your God. Of all the people on the earth, the Lord your God has chosen you to be His own special treasure." So, friend, I want you to hear me when I say that God loves you. No doubt you've heard these words before. But have you truly considered what these three words really mean? The God who made the stars in the heavens, the God who made the mountains and the seas, loves you—right where you are, just as you are. God loves you.

It's hard to grasp how a holy, perfect, infinite God could ever love sinful, unholy, imperfect, and finite people, but He does. The Bible says that God even loved us first, before we knew anything about love or were capable of love: "This is love: not that we loved God, but that he loved us" (1 John 4:10a NIV). This is a landmark passage because it gives us a clear definition of love. Contrary to our culture's way of thinking, love is not a feeling or deep emotion. Love is not a sexual attraction. Love is not a palpitating heart or sweaty palms. Love is a person, defined as God Himself. "Beloved, let us love one another. For love is of God; and everyone that loveth is born of God and knoweth God. He that loveth not, knoweth not God; for God is love. (1 John 4:7-8 KJV).

Our understanding of love is so much different than the way God loves us. Human love is temperamental, temporary, and tentative. God's love, on the other hand, is constant, eternal, unabashed, and overflowing. While we know about love, we cannot know the fullness of love until we know the One who *is* Love Himself.

God's love is perfect and meets us where we are—the good and the bad, our strengths and our weaknesses—and He loves us just the same. His love is perfect and extraordinary in every way. God loves you more passionately than any human ever could. You might think of yourself as an unimportant, nameless face in a crowd of millions, but your heavenly Father delights in you and knows you intimately. He loves you just as much as He loves His own Son, Jesus. What a great truth this is! Don't just hear this with your ears; embrace it with your heart.

When I was in the third grade, I got my first love letter from a boy in my class. When I unfolded the letter and began to read, this is what it said:

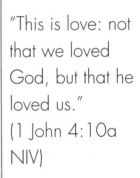

"This is love: not that we loved God, but that he loved us."
(1 John 4:10a NIV)

13

> Dear Babbie,
> I love you.
> Do you love me?
> Yes or no?
> Circle one.
> —Billy

I don't remember how I responded to Billy's third grade proposition, but I do remember how it made me feel: preferred, uniquely chosen, special. It may have just been a third-grade crush, but I can clearly recall how it felt to know someone loved me—even enough to tell me so.

The Bible is God's love letter to you. From cover to cover, He's calling your name and desires to write His love story on the tablets of your heart. Oh yes, from the first *hallelujah* to the last *amen*, God is singing your victory song. Can you hear it? Listen with your heart and experience God's eternal and passionate love for you.

Read About His Love

Near the end of Jesus' earthly mission, just before He is arrested and the road to the cross is set in motion, Jesus prays for his disciples and his followers. His prayer reveals so much about God's deep love for us.

Read John 17. In verse 20, for whom does Jesus say he is praying?

In verses 22-23 Jesus says, "I have given these people the glory that you gave me so that they can be one, just as you and I are one. I will be in them and you will be in me so that they will be completely one. Then the world will know that you sent me and that you loved them just as much as _____ _____ _____" (NCV).

Did you catch that? Jesus is praying that His followers would know that God loves them as much as God loves Jesus. He is praying that you would know and understand this great and powerful truth.

Now do you believe that you are indeed God's favorite? Write your thoughts below.

What does verse 26 tell you about God's love in and for you?

You may have memorized John 3:16 or at least heard the verse before. As you reflect today on just how much God loves you, fill in the blanks with your name and then read the verse out loud to yourself a few times:

For God so loved _____ that he gave his only begotten Son, that [if] _____believes in Him [_____] should not perish but have everlasting life. (NKJV)

Nothing could ever keep God from loving you!

Now, read the verse out loud again, emphasizing the word so. Think about the meaning and context of the word in this verse as you read the definition of the word so: "To a great extent or degree; very, extremely; exceedingly, enormously, tremendously. To an immeasurable degree." God *so* loves you.

In case you might think that you are unlovable or that you are not worthy of God's deep, unconditional love for you, let me share with you Romans 8:38-39 from *THE MESSAGE*: "I'm absolutely convinced that nothing—nothing living or dead, angelic or demonic, today or tomorrow, high or low, thinkable or unthinkable—absolutely *nothing* can get between us and God's love because of the way that Jesus our Master has embraced us" (emphasis added).

List below the things in your life that you think might make God love you less. Then, list the problems that you face—the mountain-sized trials, challenges, and tribulations that make you wonder how you'll make it through. When you have finished your lists, write over those words *NOTHING* in giant letters.

Nothing could ever keep God from loving you! Believe that promise today. You are a favored child of the Living God.

Pray About His Love

Talk to God throughout the day. Meditate on His great love for you. Repeatedly thank Him for the great love that He lavishes on you. Ask Him to increase your understanding of His love and help you to love Him more.

Dear heavenly Father,

I am overwhelmed by how much You love me. What a blessing it is to know that being a recipient of Your love doesn't depend on me. I could never do anything to earn Your love. It is a free gift. So today, anew and afresh, I will receive Your gift of love and enjoy it. I know it's not about me. It's about what You, through Your precious Son, Jesus, did for me. It's so good to know that nothing I have ever done or ever could do will separate me from Your love. Today, regardless of how I feel, I will live like the child of God I know that I am. Help me, Lord, to never take this powerful truth for granted. In Jesus' name. Amen.

Be About His Love

Have you ever noticed that love is contagious? Ask God to use you to perpetuate His love, allowing His compassion to spread from person to person, touching lives and changing hearts.

How can your love walk with God cause others to experience His love through you?

Where have you seen God's love in action today?

How can you express love for others today out of the abundant love God has lavished on you?

How is your life changed because of God's love for you?

What part of today's reading is resonating in your heart and mind right now?

Invite God to help you grow in the love and knowledge of His love for you.

DAY 2: YOU CAN START AGAIN

If any man be in Christ, he is a new creature: old things are passed away;
behold, all things are become new.
2 Corinthians 5:17 KJV

Think About His Love

Have you ever come to the point where you were just sick and tired of the situation you were in? Have you ever come to a place in your life where you needed to start over? We have all been there, and the truth is that in Christ, you can always begin again. Let me tell you my begin-again story and see if it resonates in your heart.

I was raised by parents who loved God and dedicated their lives in service to Him. I accepted Christ as a young girl and was involved in a lot of church activities growing up. I sang in the choir and later played the piano and directed the choir in my pastor-father's growing church.

I was an excellent student, hung out with other nice Christian kids, and even worked a part-time job after school. But as I reached my late teenage years and graduated from high school, my heart began to wander, and my walk with God began to suffer. As a freshman at a nearby community college I met new friends who convinced me to hang out in places I had never hung out before. In the past, Saturday nights had been spent at home with family preparing for early Sunday church services. But my new friends wanted me to party with them in bars and clubs.

Although the taste of alcohol never appealed to me, I put on a façade, even to the point of faking it, for fear of looking foolish—like a square peg in a round hole. Hanging out in the smoky, noisy bars didn't appeal to me either, but I so wanted to be accepted and to fit in. I thought this was the price I would have to pay to get signed by a record company like Motown Records and become an overnight R&B singing sensation.

God will help you and give you not only a second chance, but as many as you need to get it right.

When the club's house band would take their breaks during intermissions, my friends would urge me to go to the piano and sing. I was happy to oblige. I sat behind the old upright piano situated under the bright spotlights on that smoke-filled bar room platform. I longed for these moments, belting out the soulful melodies and lyrics of Aretha Franklin, Gladys Knight, and Roberta Flack. I wanted that applause and the cheers that came.

After a while, partying and singing in the bar on Saturday nights and then playing for Dad's church on Sunday morning began to wear on my heart. Every time I would walk into the club on Saturday nights, pangs of guilt would grip my heart like a vice because I knew that "light" could have no fellowship with "darkness" (2 Corinthians 6:14). Then on Sunday mornings, while singing gospel songs, I'd wrestle with the clutches of conviction when I recalled my actions the night before. My heart became divided and I no longer could really be at peace in either situation.

Deep inside, compromise was ruling my life. Restless with guilt and anxiety, I realized I was a hypocrite. I was not walking the walk or talking the talk. Ultimately, I felt isolated and alone.

Does hearing my story make you think of your own? Got failures from your past? Can you see the vivid details of your life's story that reveal selfish decisions to do things your own way? Have you taken a wrong turn somewhere along the way that led to some bad decisions?

It doesn't matter who you are or what your story may be. Jesus will forgive every mistake, and He can satisfy every longing, if you ask Him. Everybody can use a do-over every now and then: another opportunity to get things right with the Lord. Life in Christ is the only road to discovering what true life really is. Jesus promises the forgiveness you need, the peace you long for, the acceptance you crave, and the love you desperately hunger for.

As I began to turn my life around, I applied to a four-year Christian university in a nearby city. I got a full-ride music scholarship and earned a position as lead singer in a new Christian singing group. I found new friends who loved God, who would build up, not tear down, my faith walk. A year later I recorded my first Christian music project that included some of my own original songs. The university sent me on the road as an ambassador to visit other schools and churches and tell them about my school and my faith in Jesus Christ.

I had compromised my faith and strayed far away, but God is loving and gracious. He came to get me. I'm living proof that He uses people with a past.

God knows your story and chooses you anyway! God will help you and give you not only a second chance, but as many as you need to get it right. Your brand-new start is just a prayer away.

As you go about your work, play, and worship, remind yourself of God's desire to be lovingly involved in your life and His promise to take care of you in each circumstance. Remember, if it concerns you, then it is a situation in which God wants to reveal Himself. It is God's desire to heal whatever is broken in your life.

It doesn't matter who you are or what your story may be. Jesus will forgive every mistake and satisfy every longing—if you ask Him. No matter how many mistakes you've made, with Jesus, you can always start over!

Read About His Love

Not one of us is perfect.

Read Romans 3:23 and fill in the blanks:

"For all have _____ and _____ _____of the glory of God" (NKJV).

Every human being who has walked the face of the earth, except for Jesus Christ, has sinned and fallen short of the glory of God. We all have a past or a season of rebellion or a moment of indiscretion or a private struggle. We are not alone in our struggle. God wants to free us from the trial and lead us to fullness of life in Him. He will never reject us but will always invite us to bring our struggles to Him.

Jesus said,

"Are you tired? Worn out? Burned out on religion? Come to me. Get away with me and you'll recover your life. I'll show you how to take a real rest. Walk with me and work with me—watch how I do it. Learn the unforced rhythms of grace. I won't lay anything heavy or ill-fitting on you. Keep company with me and you'll learn to live freely and lightly."

Matthew 11:28-30 *THE MESSAGE*

What kind of life does Jesus offer in these verses?

Read 2 Corinthians 5:17. Make a list of the old things in your life that are "passed away."

Now make a list of the things in your life that are "become new."

One of the most well-known passages of Scripture is Jesus' words to a woman caught in adultery who is about to be stoned.

Read John 8:1-11. What sin did this woman have in her past?

What did Jesus say to the crowd?

What did Jesus say to the woman in verses 10-11?

Pay close attention to Jesus' words, "neither do I condemn you." We do such a good job of beating ourselves up and writhing in guilt when Jesus wants to free us from such pain. Whatever is in our past is past. Jesus calls us to turn from the past and walk together with Him into the future.

Pray About His Love

As you talk to God throughout the day, ask the Lord to free you from any guilt you carry about a "past life." Invite the Lord to shine His purifying light into the secret places in your heart to help you overcome even the most hidden sins.

Dear heavenly Father,

I am so grateful that You are the God of second chances. Thank You for another opportunity to walk in Your love—another opportunity to please You with my life. Forgive me for trying to fix things on my own. I desperately need You. I always have needed You; I just didn't know how much until now. I don't want You to be an outsider or stranger in my life. Like the great hymn writer Francis Ridley Havergal said, "Take my life and let it be, consecrated, Lord, to Thee." I make You first priority in my life. Please take Your rightful place. In Jesus' name. Amen.

Be About His Love

Maybe you don't have a dramatic story of having walked away from God, but you might have stalled in your growth or lost your zeal for a life that is totally devoted to Christ. In what ways do you feel a pull to start over today? Maybe a broken friendship needs another attempt at reconciliation. Maybe a halted prayer life needs a renewed commitment. Maybe your family is going a million different directions and you need to reset with regular family prayer. Whatever your need for starting over may be—whether it's a rededication of your life to Christ or a promise to deepen your walk with Him—reflect on it now.

What fresh start do you need to make today? Write a prayer below, offering your fresh start to God and inviting Him to give you strength and courage.

Day 3: Guard and Tend Your Heart

Above all else, guard your heart, for it is the wellspring of life.
Proverbs 4:23 NIV

Think About His Love

No one knows what starting over means better than a farmer. Whenever a farmer wants to plant a new field of crops at the beginning of a brand-new season, there are many things that he knows he must do to guarantee a successful harvest. Jesus uses the art of comparison as He tells the story of the sower or farmer in Matthew 13. He tells of a farmer who cast some seeds that fell on different types of ground. Some of the seeds fell on the path and the birds ate the seeds right up. Some seeds fell in the rocks and sprang up quickly, but had no roots to sustain them. Some fell in the thorns and got choked by the weeds. The rest of the seeds fell on good soil and yielded a harvest. You might have already guessed that Jesus isn't just talking about agriculture here; He's talking about our hearts.

Every human being is born with a heart condition. We know in our heads what good choices are, but our hearts can grow hardened to the things of God. We all make decisions to do things our own way, perceiving in our hearts that we know best. This is why Proverbs 4:23 tells us, "Above all else, guard your heart, for it is the wellspring of life" (NIV). Isn't that so true? If we want to experience life abundantly, we must continually guard, protect, and maintain our hearts by going to the One from whom real life flows—Jesus. I think farmers have a heads-up when it comes to understanding this process.

I don't know a whole lot about soil, seeds, and farming conditions. What little I do know, I have learned by observing my husband. Charles is not a commercial farmer, but he is a serious farmer. He can hardly wait to get his hands in the dirt when the early spring season comes around. For more than three decades I have observed how my husband goes through the annual task of preparing and tending his huge vegetable garden. Long before he plants a single seed in the garden, Charles prepares the soil. By tilling the soil, the ground is loosened and aerated, turning over useless debris such as weeds, rocks, and old vegetation. I have watched him go up and down each row of impacted soil, laid bare and hardened by the harsh winds of winter. The tiller turns over the soil, exposing it to fresh air, moisture, and sunshine—the very things it needs to grow and thrive.

Have you ever sensed your heart becoming hardened by life's blows? When our poor decisions coupled with sin that we can't seem to give up threaten our relationship with Jesus, we have to do the work of turning the soil. Keep remembering that God's Word cannot take root in us and flourish if we don't guard our hearts with every means possible. The process of growing up spiritually doesn't just happen routinely or mindlessly. It requires a decision on your part. You must decide for yourself that you need to grow and change. You have to decide that your heart is not available to the things of this world, but only to the life-giving God you love. No one can make that decision for you. You must determine in your own heart that you want, more than anything, to live a life that is pleasing to God. Along with this, you must make a conscious effort to submit to Him and change.

My sweet friend, if you are standing at a distance from God, decide at this very moment that you will draw near to Him. James 4:8 says, "Come close to God and God will come close to you. Wash your hands, you sinners; purify your hearts for your loyalty is divided between God and the world" (NLT). You must come to the place where what used to sustain you is no longer enough—where you know it cannot carry you through to the new season of life you long for. Remember that the Lord Jesus is as close as the mention of His name. In Jeremiah 29:12-13, the Lord invites you to call on Him. "In those days when you pray, I will listen. If you look for me wholeheartedly, you will find me" (NLT).

Just as it is with Charles' garden, so it is within your own heart. God wants you to grow. He desires that you would be "mature and complete, lacking in nothing" (James 1:4 NKJV). He wants to give you more of Himself. He wants you to bear fruit. The key to growth and maturity is diligence. I call it good, old-fashioned stick-to-it-iveness.

Once, during the gardening season, Charles had a problem with deer. They were having a field day with his field peas. One weekend, while we were on the road doing a concert, the deer came in and nibbled a portion of Charles' tender crop of peas right down to the ground. Charles was disgusted by the damage they had done. His buddies who are also farmers offered suggestions. "Put a sofa in your pea patch," one of them said. Another neighbor suggested, "Yeah, and go to the barber and get some hair and sprinkle the hair on the sofa. And while you're at it, sprinkle some cologne on the sofa." The idea was that the human and man-made scents would frighten away the deer. Still another friend said, "Put a radio in the pea patch and turn it to a hard rock station. The deer don't like the noise. That'll keep them out."

The next weekend, before we left for another concert (Charles goes on the road with me and helps me), Charles did all that his farmer friends had suggested. When we got home the following Monday, we immediately went to inspect the garden and found that the deer had come in and ravaged the entire pea patch and most of his watermelon crop. I think I saw a tear well up in my husband's eyes. Later that day, I heard Charles on the phone telling one of his friends about the damage the deer had done. He said, "I can see those deer now, having a party in my garden. I'll bet they were sitting on the sofa, smelling good, getting haircuts, and dancing to the music on the radio."

Charles had to laugh to keep from crying. But he got smart. He planted more peas and watermelons. He also put up a tall chain-link fence around the perimeter of his garden. That kept the deer out once and for all!

In the same way, you must put up a spiritual fence around your heart, guarding it against the intrusion of the enemy. You must guard your love walk with Jesus at all costs and tend to it with all diligence. It must remain first place in your life. If you open the door to compromise, a toehold becomes a foothold, and then a foothold becomes a stronghold. Don't let your love for God grow cold. You never want to get so used to Jesus that you lose the awe and wonder of knowing Him. On a moment-by-moment basis, keep giving Jesus first place in your heart and life. Make Him top priority, guarding your heart as if your life depended on it . . . because it does.

Read About His Love

Jesus once told a parable about seed falling on different kinds of soil.

Read Matthew 13:1-9, 18-23 and answer the following questions:

What happened to the seeds on the path?

What happened to the seeds in the rocks?

What happened to the seeds in the thorns?

What happened to the seeds on the good soil?

Would you say your heart is more like the path, the rocks, the thorns, or the good soil today? Why?

How can you till the soil of your heart so that God's Word can sink in deep and grow roots that produce an abundant harvest of love, faith, joy, and life?

Pray About His Love

As you talk to God throughout the day, ask the Lord to replace any stubbornness in you with a tender heart, "good soil" that gives room for His Word to take root and grow. Pray that God will protect your heart from the enemy and keep you strong to tend the soil of your heart.

Dear heavenly Father,
Sometimes my heart is like the path and the enemy snatches away my joy before I even notice it's missing. Sometimes my heart is like the rocky ground: I get a burst of zeal that quickly fades away. Sometimes my heart is like the thorns and I allow everything else to crowd in around You until my walk with You is choked out all together. Forgive me Lord, for not guarding and tending my heart. Show me how to be open and yielded to Your tender, loving care. Give me the strength and the diligence to keep my heart focused on You and to spend time in Your word and in prayer, tending the soil. Produce an abundant harvest in me and let Your love grow through me and out of me into the world. In Jesus' name. Amen.

Be About His Love

Tending your heart requires intentionality. Here are some questions and steps to guide you.

What are some ways you have tended to your heart and your walk with God in the past?

What practices help you feel most connected to God?

Write your most common daily routine in the space below and look for spaces in this routine where you could devote a few minutes to prayer, Bible study, or journaling about God's loving embrace. For example, perhaps you might pause for a few moments to read or pray while the coffee is brewing, in the midst of getting ready for the day, or as part of your bedtime routine.

Think about your life over the last week. What are the struggles that felt like deer coming to steal your growth? Circle those that apply; write in any additional struggles.

Stress
Hurt feelings
Worry
A broken relationship
Secret sin that you can't give up
Other:

Read Proverbs 4:23 and write a prayer, inviting the Lord to build a fence around your heart to keep out the intruders who threaten to wreck your chance at growth and flourishing:

Above all else, guard your heart, for it is the wellspring of life. (Proverbs 4:23 NIV)

DAY 4: YOU MATTER TO GOD

"Before I formed you in the womb I knew you, before you were born I set you apart."
Jeremiah 1:51 NIV

25

Think About His Love

I once had a conversation with a young lady who told me that although she knows God loves her, she still struggles with feelings of insignificance. She shared with me that she was verbally abused growing up. She said, "I still hear those words over and over again in my mind, playing like a tape recorder on repeat: 'You're hopeless. You're worthless. You're helpless. You're useless. You're weak and insignificant. You're damaged goods. You'll never amount to anything.'"

I prayed with this young woman who had been emotionally damaged by careless words. After we prayed, the Lord prompted me to ask her a question. I said, "If you were sitting in your car and a tape was playing something that you just couldn't stand, what would you do?" She replied, "I'd take the tape out and put in something else!" Immediately, I affirmed her answer and said, "Absolutely! And that's what you must do in this case. You must press the eject button. Remove the tape. Destroy it, so it can never be heard again. Then you must replace the tape."

Let me pause here to say that if you were ever told cruel and heartless lies such as the ones this precious sister described to me, it was wrong. If there are people in your life who either are or have been mean and hard to please, hear me: Do not confuse what they have said about you with what God says about you. And do not confuse how they feel about you with how God sees you: You are loved. You are treasured. You are accepted. You are redeemed. You are gifted. You are unequalled. You are preferred. You are blessed. You are favored.

You are of great significance to God. You are not an accident or an afterthought. You are not illegitimate, a mistake, a slipup, or an "oops." Your parents may not have been expecting you, but God always planned on it. In His eyes there are no illegitimate births. Everything that God made, He made for a reason and said it was "good." This includes you.

God can never, ever make a mistake. It was God's divine plan that you would make your debut on the planet exactly when you did. Long before you were a gleam in your father's eye, you were fashioned in the heart of God. Ages before you took your first breath, God knew the time and date of your birth, the shape of your nose, and the texture of your hair. He knew the address of the house where you would grow up and how many years you would live on the earth.

God created you because He loves you, and He wants to express His great love for the world through you. Try to wrap your mind around that truth for a moment. *The God of the universe created you intentionally, with a purpose and destiny in mind, so that He could love you, be loved by you, and express His love through you.*

The power behind your very existence is the dynamic force of God's love. He wants to do extraordinary, unbelievable things both in your life and through your life. The color of your skin could be brown, white, or yellow; you could be rich or poor. It doesn't matter if you were born in the ghetto, in the suburbs, or in some remote part of the world. It makes no difference whether or not you have a college education. You could be the mom of preschoolers or the CEO of a high-powered corporation. You could work in a factory, wait tables in a restaurant, or be unemployed. You could live in a nice house or be homeless. Your life is important to God, and your role in this world is significant. You may never be a household name or have a park or street named after you, but your life has meaning and worth. You have a destiny to fulfill. No one could ever take your place.

Everything about you is important to God. He is interested in each intricate detail of your life. If something matters to you, then it matters to God. Your relationships, finances, and job situations are of utmost concern to Him. Your health problems, family concerns, and apprehensions for the future all matter to God. You may feel unimportant or even insignificant. But God says you have always been important and significant.

The Bible says that even before God made the world, He found pleasure in loving and choosing you! Western culture says in order for you to matter in life, you have to be famous—even if it's just for sixty seconds on the Internet. This curious mindset drives people to stand out and make some noise. Not so in God's economy. Even people nobody else notices get recognition from God.

The enemy will cause you to become confused and to question everything concerning your worth. He will tell you that you don't matter— that you are damaged goods and that no one loves you, let alone God. But consider the truth: before you were born you mattered to God. That is a promise that cannot be undone by the lies of the enemy. Whether you are sitting in your kitchen, lying in a hospital room, or pacing in a prison cell, it doesn't matter. Why? Because you matter to God. Everything that pertains to you—your thoughts, words, and actions; your joys, challenges, and more—is of great importance to Him.

> Everything about you is important to God.

Read About His Love

Many of the characters we read about in the Bible felt unimportant, insignificant, or incapable. Take Jeremiah, for example.

Read Jeremiah 1:1-10 and answer the following questions:

What was the word from God that Jeremiah received?

What excuses did Jeremiah have for why he was not a good choice?

27

How did God encourage and empower Jeremiah to complete the work God called him to?

Jeremiah is a great example of the ways that we dismiss our God-given call because of our lack of understanding. You see, the more we understand about God's great love for us, the more we believe that He makes us worthy to receive it, and we are capable of going to great lengths to do that which He calls us to do.

What words describe your self-talk when you consider whether you really matter? Circle those that apply.

Too quiet
Too loud
Too heavy
Too skinny
Strayed too far for God to be able to use
Not smart enough
Don't have enough faith
Not pretty enough
Not popular enough
Not articulate or creative enough
Not _____ enough

If you are not convinced of God's overwhelming love for you—even you—look with me at Psalm 139.

Read the entire psalm and then write your name, she, or her in the appropriate blanks in the selected verses below:

You saw _____'s bones being formed
  as _____ took shape in _____ mother's body.
When _____ was put together there,
  you saw _____'s body as it was formed.
All the days planned for _____
  were written in your book
  before _____ was one day old. (NCV)

From the beginning of time itself, God had a plan to love you; you mattered even then.

Read Ephesians 1:4-5 (NLT) below and underline words that tell you that you matter to God.

Even before he made the world, God loved us and chose us in Christ to be holy and without fault in his eyes. God decided in advance to adopt us into his own family by bringing us to himself through Jesus Christ. This is what he wanted to do, and it gave him great pleasure.

Pray About His Love

Realizing our worth to God feels like an impossible calculation. How could we matter to such a great God? Sweet Friend, remember that the Bible is God's love letter to you, and all through it He is telling you that you matter to Him. And not only that, but God lovingly formed you and treasures you. Pray today for the strength to believe that you indeed matter to God.

Dear Father God,

Thank You for helping me understand more clearly just how much You love me and that Your love is greater than all my faults. Knowing that I matter to You brings me a great deal of comfort, joy, and security. It boggles my mind to know that no matter how many mistakes I make, if I confess my sins according to 1 John 1:9, You are faithful and just to forgive me and cleanse me from all unrighteousness. Lord, I want to bring You glory in all I say and do today. Help me to remember that my main goal in life is to please You—my audience of One. In the name of Jesus I pray. Amen.

Be About His Love

All that God created, He made on purpose, with purpose, and for a purpose, including you. In His great wisdom and power, He knew exactly what He was doing when He created you. As you go about your day, remember that you exist because God loves you and finds great pleasure and delight in you. Everything about you, and all that concerns you, is important to God.

Drawing upon today's reading, write some "I Matter" statements and read them out loud to yourself.

> All that God created, He made on purpose, with purpose, and for a purpose.

29

I matter to God because

_____.

I matter to God because

_____.

I matter to God because

_____.

As you reflect on this great truth that you matter to God, consider how you might speak a word of hope to a brother or sister today. Could you speak one kind word or do one act of kindness toward someone you come in contact with today? Let someone know that he or she matters to you because you see him or her through the eyes of faith and love.

In the space below, write some names of people who need to know that they matter to God and pray for them by name. Ask God to give you the rights words at the right time to bless them with the truth that they matter to God.

DAY 5: GOD KNOWS YOUR NAME

"He calls his own sheep by name and leads them out."
John 10:3b NRSV

Think About His Love

When I was little, I loved to watch the children's show _Romper Room_. At the conclusion of each episode, the host would bring out her Magic Mirror. She'd hold that mirror up to the camera as if she could actually see every child who was sitting in front of the television, and she would look into the mirror and greet all her friends who were watching in television land. Then she would begin to call them by name. In a very sweet and inviting way she'd say, "I see Lisa, and I see Joey... ...hello, Fran! Happy Birthday to you, Susan. Have a great vacation, Laurie."

Every time I'd tune in to that wonderful program, I would make sure I leaned in and got closer to her at the end of the show. I listened very attentively in case that nice lady

called my name. But she never did. As a child, I wondered for the longest time why I was never recognized. Didn't she know I was watching her show? Wasn't she aware that I had a birthday too?

Then one day I had an epiphany. One day I made a connection. I figured out that sending in a postcard with my name, address, city, and state printed on it would probably increase the chances of getting my name called. But until I figured that out, I yearned just to have that sweet lady call my name. I longed for her to recognize me.

Have you ever just wanted to be noticed, but instead you were overlooked? Being ignored and rejected hurts, doesn't it? I know how you feel. Even more than that, Jesus knows how you feel. The prophet Isaiah described the plight of the Son of God with these words: "He was despised and rejected by men; a man of sorrows, and acquainted with grief; and as one from whom men hide their faces he was despised, and we esteemed him not" (Isaiah 53:3, RSV).

Although others may fail to recognize you, God sees you. He takes notice. He not only knows your name but He calls your name. Let me tell you about another kid who got overlooked—by some, but not by all. The story of the boy whose lunch would feed a crowd of five-thousand is a favorite to preachers, songwriters, and storytellers alike. It has become quite famous, in fact. This child's part in the miracle that Jesus performed played a significant role in the Lord's earthly ministry.

Many details are brought to light in the story. We read about the location and how many people were there. We read about the time of year that it was, and in some Gospel accounts, what time of day it was. But one detail is missing. We don't know the name of the lad who brought his food—two fish and five loaves—to Jesus.

He was just a young boy on his way to who knows where, when he was asked to share everything he had to eat. *We don't know his name, but God does.* This nameless lad handed his fish and bread to Andrew, Simon Peter's brother, that day. And the lives of five thousand men, besides women and children, were changed forever. One nameless little boy was able to participate in the ministry of the Lord Jesus because of one simple act of obedience. Even today, more than two millennia after the fact, we are still telling the story of this cooperative little boy, and God is still receiving the glory.

Bread and fish are such simple elements. But little is much whenever God is involved. And I can just image Father God leaning over the balcony of heaven, smiling as only He could when that small, simple meal became a supernatural banquet for a multitude. I can just imagine God turning to the "great cloud of witnesses," saying, "That's my boy." And when Jesus lifted up the loaves and fish to give thanks, knowing how much children delighted Him, I'd like to think He included that young lad in His prayer of thanks.

Somewhere in the annals of time, God has recorded the name of that little fellow, just like He has recorded other people in the Bible who have gone nameless...like the woman at the well in Samaria (John 4:7), the woman with the issue of blood (Luke 8:43), and the woman caught in adultery (John 8:4).

You were created to bring God glory with your life.

People may not always notice you. But *people* often miss seeing the bigger picture. *With God, everyone is important.* Every good deed is significant, and no one goes unnoticed. If there have been times when you responded in faith to God, and it seemed people around you didn't acknowledge or even appreciate it, know that God never takes you for granted. God is pleased when your life demonstrates His love, even when others don't seem to notice.

Just think about it. Here we are still talking about this young, nameless boy. I cannot help but believe God wants you to know, even when people fail to recognize you, He's looking your way. And when Father God takes notice of an act of kindness, He always remembers. He looks your way because He loves you. Each time you follow His lead in faith it is recorded in His heavenly archives. God will make sure you are rewarded for returning His embrace—either in this life or the life to come.

Even though your boss may not pat you on the back for the good job you're doing, God applauds you. No one may have noticed that you stood during your bus ride home so an older lady could take a seat. But God observed how you put the comforts of another ahead of your own. Your kids might forget to say thank you for waiting in the long carpool lines, but your Father is pleased with your efforts. Your generosity pleases God and demonstrates His love to those around you.

Living to please God is the primary reason you were born. If you can truly understand this powerful principle, you will never again wonder whether or not you are seen, known, and making a difference. As a matter of fact, when you understand the powerful truth that you were created to bring God glory with your life, you will never again ask the question, "Does my life matter?" You can know, without a doubt, that you are significant. Your life is a precious treasure to a loving God.

Read About His Love

Let's look more closely at the story of this boy who shared his lunch.

Read John 6:1-13 and answer the following questions:

What sea did Jesus cross (v. 1)?

Who followed Jesus (v. 2)?

Where did Jesus go (v. 3)?

Was Jesus standing or sitting (v. 3)?

What time of year was it (v. 4)?

How does your Bible translation refer to the boy (v. 9)?

How does the passage describe the land in the area (v. 10)?

How many people were there (v. 10)?

What did Jesus do with the food (v. 11)?

What was the miracle (vv. 12-13)

This story is packed with specific details about who, what, where, when, how, and why, but the name of the boy doesn't make it into the Bible. You know, sometimes we have to surrender the desire to hear our name called by people because we know that the God of the universe knows our name. Even when we are one of the main characters in a situation, we may not get any recognition. But God sees our faithfulness and knows our name. We can take comfort in knowing that God sees us, knows us, calls us by name, and uses us for His good purposes.

Like the boy's lunch, we too have something that God can multiply to bless people.

What is in your "basket" that God can use?

Pray About His Love

Keep in mind today that God is concerned about every area of your life. He is interested in your family, your work, your relationships—everything that brings you joy or breaks your heart. He sees each tear you cry. He rejoices with every celebration. He hears you and comes quickly when you call. Pray throughout this day to become more aware of your being known by the Maker of the whole world.

Dear heavenly Father,

Thank You for knowing me and for loving me so perfectly. Help me to let go of any desire I have for recognition; may everything about my life point only to You. I know that You know me and call me by name; I don't need to be called out by others. Father, use me like the boy in the miraculous story of the feeding of the five thousand. Use what I have to bless a multitude. I will give You all the praise and glory. In Jesus' name. Amen.

Be About His Love

God knows your name. This realization should fill you with praise!

Write your name vertically in the space below. Beside each letter of your name, write a word of praise that begins with that letter. As you go about your day, let every letter of your name, every word on your lips, every breath from your lungs be an act of praise to the God who made you, knows you, and calls you.

Week 1

VIDEO VIEWER GUIDE

Promise #1: You are loved _____ by God.

He loves you without _____ and without _____.

God's love is _____.

"For God so loved _____, that he gave his only begotten Son,

that [if] _____ believeth in him _____ should

not perish, but have everlasting life."

John 3:16 KJV

God's   love   is   _____   and   _____

_____.

You can _____ _____.

You _____ to God.

Week 2

YOU ARE BEAUTIFUL TO GOD

When God created the heavens and the earth and everything they encompassed, He proclaimed it was all good—and this includes you. How so? Before you were conceived in your mother's womb, you were in the mind of God. To Him, you will always be beautiful. You are His masterpiece.

There is no television commercial, magazine ad, or human opinion that can change this fact. You don't need anyone's approval or validation. The only thing that matters is what God says about you. If God says you are beautiful, favored, chosen, blessed, and free, then it is so. Now, it's time for you to believe it *completely*. From the very beginning you have been a part of God's great big, beautiful love story!

This week you will discover that when God looks at you, He sees you as beautiful. You may look in the mirror and see your failures, disappointments, unfulfilled expectations, trial-worn lines around your eyes, and the years of pain just below the surface. But God sees you, beautiful you. As you go about your week and soak in the daily readings, meditate on this: *Everything God made is beautiful—including me.*

Scripture Memorization

This week you will continue focusing on our memory verse, John 17:23 (NCV):

"I will be in them and you will be in me so that they will be completely one. Then the world will know that you sent me and that you loved them just as much as you loved me."

Continue using the index cards in visible places and reading the verse when you get up, throughout the day, and as you go to bed. Remember that another great way to memorize Scripture is to write or type it.

DAY 1: YOU ARE VALIDATED

Jesus answered and said unto her, "Whoever drinketh of this water shall thirst again;
But whosoever drinketh of the water that I shall give him shall never thirst; but the
water that I shall give him shall be in him a well of water springing
up into everlasting life."
John 4:13-14 KJV

Think About His Love

A genuine concern today is identity theft. Millions of people are victims of this serious crime on an annual basis. Identity theft occurs when personal and private information is stolen in order to commit a fraudulent crime. The person committing the crime gains access to bank accounts and potentially steals social security numbers and an abundance of private and confidential information.

The term *identity theft* was coined around 1964, but identity theft is nothing new. Your adversary, satan, has been on a mission to steal the identity of anyone who will allow him to do it. And he has been stealing from the beginning of time. John 10:10 says, "The thief's purpose is to steal and kill and destroy" (NLT). It's his agenda to steal your hopes, kill your dreams, and destroy your future. But praise God for Jesus! He said, "My purpose is to give them a rich and satisfying life" (John 10:10 NLT). This is the kind of life Jesus desires for you to experience—a life that is overflowing with potential and fulfilling in every way.

God has placed His stamp of approval on your life. Bear with me as I briefly reflect on something we touched on last week (day 4), this time more deeply and from a slightly different perspective—because life is much this way. Let's ponder this together. Have you ever been told things such as "You'll never amount to anything.... You're ugly.... You're a failure.... You're a constant disappointment.... You have absolutely no talent.... You don't count.... You're not good enough"?

These verbal assaults and a host of others cut deep, right to the soul. Maybe one or both of your parents verbally abused you. Perhaps someone you looked up to, someone you really trusted, wounded you with careless words. And if you were told any of these things as a child, no doubt you remember specific and numerous times and places when those verbal bombs were hurled at you.

Who is the originator of these verbal assaults and the relentless, repetitive attacks you might be hearing over and over in your mind? You might say it was your dad, mom, grandparents, a teacher, a coach, your husband, or the bully on the playground. No, my friend, these people may be most immediately responsible for insulting you, but they are not the author of these destructive words. The enemy is the author of every attack, whether it is against your body, your mind, or your spirit. Remember the enemy is your adversary. He will do all he can to keep you from becoming everything God has destined you to be.

Our world is suffering from a love deficiency. Like the old songs says, "Everybody needs love." Every soul craves love. So many people today sense a void in their hearts, an acute emptiness that can only be satisfied by love.

How many of us have gotten off track by "looking for love in all the wrong places," to use the popular saying? Maybe you have looked to others at times to satisfy that empty feeling. Maybe you have searched for approval from those you thought had "that certain something" you felt you were lacking. Perhaps you have sought affirmation for the duties you perform at work. But time and again, you have been disappointed and disillusioned when you didn't get it.

The culture we live in often tells women: "You must have a husband in order to gain the approval you need." We look at the things others may possess and we conclude, "You need more money in order to feel more important." Added to this, our modern culture counsels us, "To find the love you need, look within yourself." Countless people have tried each of these things and more, only to come up empty. Some have gone beyond themselves, making tremendous sacrifices for others, inwardly trying to gain the love they think they need, but sadly, all too often they end up in the same place. Disappointed, disillusioned, and discouraged.

So, where can you find real love? Recall this with me as we continue exploring this eternal truth. Love is not a warm and fuzzy feeling. Love is not an emotional urge or even a deep desire. Love is not feeling good about yourself or someone else. Love is not a sexual drive. Love is a person, and that person is Jesus.

Stop and think about the truth—not your feelings or the opinion of someone else wrapped in flesh—but the unchanging, undeniable, absolute truth. *The love you crave and long for is embodied in one person, Jesus Christ.* He is the only one who is both qualified and able to bring real love, meaning, and purpose to your life.

No one could realize the transforming power of the love of Christ more than the woman at the well. Interestingly, John, the writer of this Gospel account, does not give her a name. But as you know, this doesn't take away from her compelling story. We don't need to know her name to identify with her circumstances.

After a slew of failed marriages, this lonely lady had become all too familiar with the pain of emotional drought. Now living with a man who was not her husband, she had paid the high cost of lowering her expectations. Added to this, she was the talk of the town. So you can imagine how keenly she felt the sting of social isolation. By the world's definition the woman who encountered Jesus at a well outside her town in Samaria was a total loser.

> The love you crave and long for is embodied in one person, Jesus Christ.

If your story is even remotely like hers, then you need to hear this: *In God's eyes there are no losers, and God's opinion of you is the only one that matters.*

Read About His Love

Let's take a closer look at a day in the life of this woman at the well—a lonely soul who was craving true love. It was a day that changed her life forever.

Read John 4:1-42.

Imagine all of the baggage that this woman had been carrying around. List it below.

Verses 4-6 set the scene for us. According to these verses, what time of day was she at the well?

Why do you think she would choose noon, the hottest part of the day?

By going to draw water in the middle of the day, she probably thought she wouldn't encounter anyone who knew about the past she kept repeating, the present pain she was enduring, or the future she was dreading. She wouldn't have to overhear the constant whispers and the continuous gossip. She wouldn't have to endure the judgmental looks and the ridicule from others in her community.

Truth be told, most, if not all, of the things people were saying about her were accurate. The gossip circulating around town about her was true. No doubt, she carried feelings of guilt in the depths of her soul that were almost more than she could bear.

What kind of emotions do you think the woman felt every moment of every day? Circle those that apply; write in any additional emotions.

Shame
Pain
Despair
Sadness
Other:

When have you carried around similar pain? What does it feel like to carry around such deep shame?

The life of this woman, who had been caught in the act, was the total sum of every past mistake and every poor choice. Life had taken its toll on her, for the weight of heavy water pots were much easier to carry than the weight of her existence. All the guilt and shame she had wrestled with over the years had whittled away her self-worth, until the only thing that remained was a small pile of rubble. She had a thirst to experience real love, joy, and peace. Yet she had concluded that such a wonderful life could never become her reality.

Read verses 10-14. What does Jesus offer this woman who is desperate for a new life?

How does the woman respond to Jesus' offer?

According to 15-20, how does the conversation take a turn?

"If you knew the gift of God and who it is that asks you for a drink, you would have asked him and he would have given you living water."
(John 4:10 NIV)

Coming face-to face with Jesus, the Messiah, would be the defining moment of her life. That very moment she met Jesus at Jacob's well would be the very moment that would change her life forever. Perhaps for the first time, she met a man who wasn't looking for what He could get from her. Jesus was longing to bless her with the love that only He could provide. She encountered someone who addressed her deepest longings and validated her true worth.

How does this woman's encounter with Jesus validate her?

In verses 39-42, how does the woman respond to this amazing encounter?

After this encounter with Jesus, this once lonely woman went home very different than when she came. She returned to her town—filled with people who had witnessed her failings and characterized her as a lost cause—changed, forgiven, and whole. Jesus went out of His way to help this "thirsty" woman, and He is still going out of His way today. Jesus' love reaches to the heights and depths of wherever you are in your journey of life. His amazing love is available to you now.

Pray About His Love

Talk to God about every broken area in your life, and ask Him to heal your brokenness. Invite Him to restore you, both to Himself and to others. Remember, Jesus is everything you need.

Dear sweet Father,

All my life I have been thirsty
For real love and joy within,
Searching in all the wrong places,
What I gained was a life of sin.

When my soul was parched and barren,
Burdened down by every care,
Hallelujah, there you found me,
And you heard your daughter's prayer.

Thank you for The Living Water,
Bread of Life, my faithful Friend,
Only You can satisfy me,
And I'll never thirst again.

In Jesus' name I pray. Amen.

Be About His Love

Like the woman at the well, each and every one of us is "thirsty" and broken in one way or another.

What do you thirst for today? Circle those that apply; write in any additional longings.

Peace
Joy
Hope
Freedom from sin
Other:

How about love? True love. Love that is deep, sure, pure, and honoring. Do you thirst for love from someone who will build you up and not tear you down? Do you want to experience a love that stays the course no matter what? Then, my dear sister, I encourage you to have a life-changing encounter with Jesus, the only person who is both qualified and able to address your deepest longings and quench your every "thirst" forever. No one can validate you like Jesus: the One who lived, died, and rose again, so that you could live loved and share this real love with others.

What is your response to Jesus' offer of living water today?

Do you find it easy to accept gifts from people but difficult to accept God's gift of unconditional love, grace, and forgiveness? Why or why not?

Who do you know who is desperate for real love, life-giving water, and true validation?

Think about some ways you might share this love with him or her, and invite God to make a way for you.

DAY 2: YOU CAN SHARE THE LIVING WATER

"Go into all the world and preach the good news to all creation."
Mark 16:15 NIV

Think About His Love

I had a conversation recently with my sweet friend, Lisa. She is a gifted singer and pianist. Lisa has a deep burden and sensitivity to the needs of hurting women in her neighborhood. She knows all too well that these women, much like the woman at the well, need to have an encounter with Jesus. They need to know that He can and will satisfy their deep hunger and insatiable thirst for true love.

Lisa opens her home to the women in her community on a bimonthly basis and invites them to brunch. She decorates her home with flowers and candles to make it feel warm and inviting. "It's not about trying to impress people," she says. Lisa makes a point to use real plates, glasses, and cloth napkins, remarking that women sense God's love through her warmth and hospitality. She asks each invited guest to bring a covered dish to share with the group.

Lisa says she wants her guests to feel loved, pampered, special, and comfortable. After they have eaten their meal, she leads the women in a time of singing and prayer and then shares a simple devotional message. She finds that the women are hungry for fellowship and connection and will often open up and share concerning the issues they face.

In this warm and safe environment, Lisa is able to pray with them. Several ladies have received Christ as Savior as a result of these gatherings. Lisa said, "One dear lady, who came as a guest with a friend, sensed the love of Jesus the moment she walked through the front door. Overwhelmed by the love of Christ, she cried the whole time she was here."

So many women are broken inside over marital issues, family crises, financial challenges, and more. Lisa uses her home as a safe haven and a beacon of light in a very dark, troubled world. She describes this effort as her labor of love.

I was humbled to learn that a song I wrote a few years ago, "Each One, Reach One," inspired Lisa to open the doors of her home and her heart. Here is the chorus of the song:

> For each one, can reach one
> As we follow after Christ
> We all can lead one
> We can lead one to the Savior
> Then together we can tell the world
> That Jesus is the Way
> If we each one, reach one*

Lisa knows all too well that women are starving for approval and a word of validation. She also understands that women often look for it in the wrong places—like the hurting woman who met Jesus at the well. I agree. Meeting the needs of hurting women is why the Lord has moved strongly upon my heart to share my story and His love in my concerts. As I go, I thank God for using people like Lisa who not only tell hurting women about Jesus, but show them His love as well.

Lisa has a final word of advice for you. If God gives you a burden to help women, then do something about it. She says, "If God gives you a vision and burden to help hurting women, He will provide the resources. God will help you carry it out. It's kind of like what happened in the movie *Field of Dreams*. 'If you build it, they will come.'"

That's what Jesus does. He builds wonderful things, and all are invited to come. He builds new expectations from dashed hopes and broken dreams. He builds a great future for ruined lives and wrecked families. He builds a strong faith for the weak, the wounded, and the outcast. He builds a fire for those who have been tossed out in the cold and a foundation of truth for those who have believed the lies of the enemy. Jesus builds trust for those who have been abused and shelters for those with no place to go. The list goes on and on. Tell me, what has Jesus built in your life?

This is good news for you, for me, and for everyone of us: Jesus can fix whatever is broken in your life. Regardless of who you are and how far you may have fallen, nothing is too hard for Jesus. No matter how many times you have loved and lost or how many times your heart has been broken—you're never too far gone or beyond repair. Step up and take a long drink from the Well that will never run dry. Jesus offers all He is for all that you are. Your deepest longing can be satisfied only as you develop an intimate relationship with Jesus Christ. Drink His living water and be certain that you will never, ever thirst again.

Read About His Love

Come to Jesus for the love you need. He is your only source of real love, and He has more than enough love to go around. Everyone has a standing invitation to come to Him.

Are you desperate for love? Read Jeremiah 31:3. What is the answer to the need for love?

Do you need acceptance? Read Ephesians 1:6b and write the verse below. Circle the words that tell you that you are accepted.

"Yes, I have loved you with an everlasting love; Therefore with loving-kindness I have drawn you." (Jeremiah 31:3 NKJV)

Don't think you're beautiful? Read Psalm 45:11 and write the verse below. Draw a picture frame around the words that tell you about your beauty.

Need a really good friend? You've found one in Jesus. Read Proverbs 18:24 and write the verse below. Draw a heart around the words that tell you that you have the best kind of friend.

Hungry for something food can't satisfy? Read John 6:35 and draw a loaf of bread around the words that speak to you of satisfying hunger.

Got an unquenchable thirst? Read John 6:37b and draw a well around the words that tell you that your thirst has been quenched.

Been rejected? Read John 6:37b. Underline twice the words that affirm your acceptance.

Think you're too bad to be forgiven? Write 1 John 1:9 below and circle the whole verse, because there is nothing you can do to keep God from forgiving you when you seek Him with your whole heart.

Pray About His Love

Today can be the start of an exciting new season in your life, knowing that Christ liberally supplies all that you need and long for. This is a story worth telling over and over. Ask God to forgive your sins, heal your brokenness, and restore you to Himself. Then, keep your heart and eyes open to the way God might be calling you to share His great love and life-giving water with those around you.

Dear heavenly Father,

You alone are the answer to my deepest longings. You satisfy my deepest need. Forgive me, Father, when I look for love, validation, and affirmation in the wrong places. Help me find my identity in You. Give me a vision for sharing Your deep love and life-giving water to those in my community. I promise to give You all the praise and the glory. In Jesus' name. Amen.

Be About His Love

Do you know anyone who is lonely, broken, or isolated? Perhaps a neighbor down the street needs a friend. Maybe someone who comes to church alone needs a little fellowship. Make it a point to reach out to a thirsty person today. Take a small gift, make eye contact, offer a hug. Invite your friend who may need a little godly validation to come with you to a special church or neighborhood event. In Christ, the opportunities are endless for you to express His real love.

Reflect on Lisa's story and consider what it would look like for women to gather every now and then to fellowship, sing, share stories, and pray together. Make some notes about whom you could work with, where you might host these gatherings, and how you would get the word out.

DAY 3: YOU ARE VINDICATED

Jesus said unto her, "Neither do I condemn thee: go, and sin no more."
John 8:11 KJV

Think About His Love

My husband, Charles, has this unique ability to fix things. I'm talking about those everyday items around the house like furniture, bicycles, basic plumbing, cars, toys, and machinery. There's definitely a very positive side to Charles's handyman ways. The man is a born recycler. He was taught as a boy, instead of throwing a broken item away, to find a way to fix it and use it again. Needless to say, Charles has carried that same philosophy

Jesus takes damaged goods . . . and gives them a new lease on life.

into our marriage. Nothing ever gets thrown away, but waits in the garage until the moment it can be reused. If you ever come to our home for a visit, I'll do my best to keep you from entering the garage. If somehow you end up out there among the tools, spare parts, compressors, and hoses, let me warn you now. You will be taking your safety into your own hands.

There is one special item that has been totally renewed under Charles's care: his prized possession, a 1951 Chevy Deluxe. Charles bought the car from our friend John. The day Charles pulled the car into our driveway I was convinced that John had gotten the better end of the deal. Hoisted up on the back of a trailer, the old car was nothing more than a big heap of metal ready for the junkyard; it was an eyesore.

Charles couldn't have been more excited. However, I was skeptical, thinking that he had bitten off more than he could chew. I tried to convince him that restoring a car was a huge, expensive undertaking. But Charles was not about to change his mind. He flashed his wide, bright smile, and my hubby's eyes twinkled like a kid on Christmas morning as he watched the old, dilapidated car roll off the trailer and into its resting place at the front of our house.

I stood there in the yard and prayed under my breath, "Lord, the thing I feared has come upon me." Our pretty, brick ranch-style house and beautifully landscaped yard were, in an instant, transformed into the neighborhood junkyard, on display for the entire world to see.

Much to my delight, over time, the car has seen a total transformation. Charles's skillful abilities and careful devotion to this car have brought a once lifeless, colorless heap of metal back to life. The 1951 Chevy Deluxe is now a beautifully restored collector's item. From the inside out, the car is stunning.

With its shiny new paint job, power steering, V-8 engine, shock absorbers, automatic transmission, compact disc player, and air-conditioning, I can't help but have a brand-new respect for this car. Lovingly called "The '51," the car is no longer an "it." Rather, it is now referred to as *she*. At my husband's skillful hands *she* has been changed from an ugly mess to a spectacular masterpiece.

Isn't this the story of redemption? Isn't this the story of anyone and everyone who has encountered the life-changing, skillful, careful touch of Jesus? I can tell you without a doubt, it is! He is a master at fixing ruined lives, repairing busted families, mending broken hearts, and shoring up dashed dreams. Like no one else can, Jesus takes damaged goods headed to the trash heap and gives them a new lease on life.

Last week we briefly touched on the story of the woman caught in the act of adultery. Today we'll look a little more closely at her story to discover the way that Jesus stands ready to give us a new lease on life, even when we've made a huge mess of our lives.

Recall that the woman was dragged out before a crowd of people, the religious leaders leading the charge, ready to stone the woman and accuse Jesus of heresy. What a beautiful story of love, genuine care, and concern Jesus exhibited for this woman who had been caught in the very act of adultery. Just think about it. A crowd of people had gathered in the temple courtyard during the early morning hours just after dawn to hear Jesus teach. Use your imagination and place yourself among the crowd. Can you see her now, frightened, embarrassed, shocked, humiliated, and ashamed?

It was bad enough that she had stooped to a new low and gotten herself involved with a man who was not her husband. But to be dragged to the temple of all places, probably with nothing more than a bed sheet wrapped around her, was definitely worse. Where was her husband anyway? Was he out of town on business? Had he already left for work? Was she in love with the man she cheated with? Did she love her husband, whom she had cheated against? Had she been seeing this man over a long period of time, or was it a one-night stand? I don't know. But one thing was certain. She was about to meet someone who cared enough to make sense of all the shadowy questions concerning her life.

Then Jesus did a strange and wonderful thing. Ignoring the Pharisees who demanded that He uphold the law, He bent down and started writing on the ground with His finger. When her accusers continued to press Jesus to grant the stoning and give her what she deserved, He stood up from the place where He had been writing and said to them, "He that is without sin among you, let him first cast a stone at her" (John 8:7b KJV).

I can hear the thud of dropping rocks now. These upholders of the law were convicted by their own lawlessness, and they went away one by one, beginning with the oldest to the youngest. Then Jesus was left alone with the woman and she was vindicated. In front of all of those people, Jesus had given her a second chance and a new life.

While Jesus had cause by law to have the woman stoned to death, He never used it against her. Anybody can take a person down by throwing stones. It takes real love to build up and restore. Jesus was the only person who was qualified to throw stones that day, yet He refused to lift a condemning hand against her. He genuinely cared for her soul. Much like what I saw in Charles's Chevy Deluxe before restoration, the crowd only saw in this woman a heap of garbage to be thrown out. But Charles saw much more than that in his car, and Jesus saw immensely more than that in this woman. He saw a priceless treasure, one who is worth dying to save. And that, dear friend, is how He feels about you.

Read About His Love

I read somewhere that women are so consumed by guilt that almost 90 percent of what we do is driven by it. As you read the story of the woman caught in adultery, imagine your own struggle with guilt and permit Jesus to free you from any feelings of condemnation.

Read John 8:2-11. Imagine what Jesus might have been writing on the ground. Write some thoughts below about the various things He could have said given the situation.

Write verses 10-11 below.

Where do you think her accusers went, and why do you think they disappeared so quickly?

How did Jesus' actions vindicate her in front of the crowd?

Consider the accusations made about you. When have you felt accused and on the verge of losing everything?

How does Jesus' life, death, and resurrection vindicate you in front of your accuser?

What does Jesus call us to do as this story ends?

To know that Jesus does not condemn me, even though I'm guilty, unlocks the door to freedom and throws away the key. Although she was a victim, she was also guilty. She knew she had committed a grievous offense. Jesus knew this, as well. But she learned something we must also come to understand. Jesus is never on a search-and-destroy mission as it concerns the Father's most-prized creations. He is interested in *saving us from our sins, not punishing us for our sins*. Jesus is always on a seek-to-save mission for lost and hurting souls.

Pray About His Love

Jeremiah 31:34b (NLT) says, "I will forgive their wickedness, and I will never again remember their sins." Praise God! Because Jesus loves you more than you know, you never again have to be consumed or controlled by guilt.

Dear heavenly Father,
You have been so good and so faithful; I just have to praise You. I confess that I have wandered far from You at times and found myself standing guilty and accused. Thank You for saving me, for restoring me, and for vindicating me before my accuser. I know I am truly blessed, Lord; make my life a blessing to someone else. In Jesus' name. Amen.

Be About His Love

Memorize John 8:11b. Every time you hear the voice of the accuser declaring your guilt and your sentence, let Jesus' words speak right into your life. Jesus said, "Neither do I condemn thee: go, and sin no more" (KJV).

Day 4: You Are Valued

"I will not leave you comfortless: I will come to you."
John 14:18 KJV

Think About His Love

Did you know that the human body is worth approximately five dollars? It is made up of inexpensive ingredients like water, oxygen, hydrogen, and carbon—but your soul is priceless! Shouldn't we care for our souls just as much as, if not more than, our bodies?

I met a woman who, after years of drug abuse and a careless sex life, was diagnosed with HIV/AIDS. She said something that I shared with you on Day 1 of this week's study.

She said,

> Identity theft is nothing new. The devil has been trying to steal my identity, kill my dreams and destroy my life for a long time. His only mission is to kill, steal, and destroy, and I almost let him do it. But, praise God, with Jesus it's never too late. Others may count you out, but Jesus didn't just give me back my old life—He gave me a brand-new life. I'm grateful for each and every day that I have been given since my diagnosis. And you know, I can really say that this has worked out for the best because this disease is what drove me to God. That was almost twenty years ago.

This transformed woman knows she should have been dead and gone, and her doctors are amazed how she has defied the odds. "It ain't nothin' but the grace of God that I'm still here," she says. "I'm a walking miracle." She's lost a few friends along the way because of her situation, but she's quick to say, "They weren't my friends to begin with. I've got too much living to do today to be worried about the past. The past is the past, and that's where I intend to keep it." She has discovered that with Christ, her life has real meaning and value.

There is another woman in the Bible who had what the King James Version describes as an "issue of blood." When I read her story, I get a glimpse of a desperate, lonely woman who was losing all sense of her identity, self-worth, and value. While Jesus was on His way to take care of someone else, we meet the woman with the "issue of blood."

Hopelessly incurable and outcast in her community, this woman had suffered with this affliction for twelve long years. She had depleted all of her money trying to find a solution for her sickness, and she was no better off twelve years after she began. As a matter of fact, she was worse. At one time, she probably was a person of financial means, but after twelve years of going from doctor to doctor, trying this potion and that notion, she found herself financially destitute. She was dead broke.

According to Mosaic law, this suffering woman was considered unclean. She was as much of an outcast as any person with leprosy. Most likely she lived outside the city walls, away from the general population, because she had to avoid contact with other people. Anyone or anything she touched would immediately be considered unclean.

For certain, this meant she had no friends who would drop by, and no relatives would fill her house with laughter on holidays. She had long forgotten the joy of giving a birthday gift to a friend or loaning a cup of sugar to a neighbor. This woman's debilitating condition meant there was no possibility for her to have an intimate marital relationship. And because of this, there was no possibility she would ever bear children. Finally, sadly, this certainly meant she could not go to the synagogue to worship God, and she so desperately needed Him. Surely, this weak and traumatized woman led an extremely lonesome, dreadful life.

So, it took a great deal of courage for her to leave home and navigate the streets to find Jesus. They were filled with people who had heard that He was passing through town. Word had spread that Jesus had healed the sick, raised the dead, and cast out evil spirits. While moving carefully among the massive crowd, she saw Jesus, the object of her hope. Weak, anemic, and afraid, she dared to reach out to touch the tassels on the hem of His garment, perhaps just brushing His cloak as He steered through the crowd. She knew that, technically, this risky move would also make Jesus unclean—but for her, this was a now-or-never, do-or-die moment. So, she reached out and touched Him.

Immediately, she knew her body was healed. Feeling the healing virtue flow out of His body, Jesus insisted on knowing who had touched Him. Shaking and afraid, only after He insisted, she came forward and confessed that she was the one. Admitting to making that desperate move, she told Jesus it was her last-ditch effort to end twelve years of misery.

I love how Jesus responded to her situation. He did not reprimand her for touching Him or scold her for touching others. He did not embarrass, rebuke, or humiliate her for breaking religious rules or for going against the cultural norms of the day. Instead, with compassion in His voice and love in His eyes, He recognized her and called her *daughter,* a term of deep love and concern. Jesus knew her need all too well, just as surely as He had felt her desperate touch.

No longer was this once-lonely woman a victim of her circumstances; she had now become a victor *over* her circumstances. Jesus had made her whole.

When Jesus recognized her faith, I believe He met all of her needs: physical, spiritual, social, and emotional. Just as Jesus had met her need for physical healing, He fulfilled her emotional need to be acknowledged. I could certainly understand that Jesus healed a void in her heart that had likely stemmed from a lack of love, validation, and human interaction.

Jesus is the absolute best at doing what He does: restoring broken lives. He masterfully heals wounded hearts, bruised bodies, and troubled minds. He perfectly restores dysfunctional families, broken fellowships, and dashed dreams.

Jesus understands well how the issues of life can compile and compress, one upon the other, year after year, until it seems there is nothing left to restore. Do you have issues that have made you retreat from the world? Did a so-called friend betray you, leaving you unable to trust? Are you housebound because of age or illness? Do you long for friendship, fellowship, and the embrace of a close friend? Do you long to experience God's embrace? Do you desire for His healing virtue to flow into your life, immediately healing the pain you've carried for years?

If you are battling against feelings of low self-esteem, you may be tempted to remain distant from God and others. But remember those destructive "arrows" of shame and insecurity come from the accuser, the enemy of your soul. Don't run from Jesus; run to Him. Go to our faithful Counselor and Master Physician. Press through the crowd, beyond your fears, and touch the hem of His garment. You are loved. You are healed. You are valued.

> Press through the crowd, beyond your fears, and touch the hem of His garment.

Read About His Love

I'll say it again: Jesus takes damaged goods that are well on their way to the trash heap and gives them a new lease on life.

Read Luke 8:41-48. What was the scene as the woman with the "issue of blood" approached Jesus?

Put a checkmark beside the words that describe the woman's situation, and add any others you might think of.

__desperate
__hopeless
__bankrupt
__despairing
__in need of a miracle
Other:

I love the way the King James Version of this Scripture includes the words "issue of blood." Other translations leave out the word issue and only mention the years of bleeding. Though "issue of blood" was a way of saying she had a flow of blood, the word issue can speak to us in another way. We all have issues, don't we? Our issues sometimes leave us broken and out of hope, but one touch from Jesus gives us healing and wholeness and a brand new start.

What "issues" are going on in your life that cause you to run to Jesus?

Write a few words in response to the healing that Jesus brings to your issues.

It had probably been years, if ever, that this woman felt valued and worth anything. But Jesus spoke to her and, in front of the crowd, named her worth and granted her wholeness.

Read verses 47-48 again. Write your name into the story and hear the Master Healer name your value and wholeness.

_____, be of good comfort; thy faith hath made thee whole; go in peace. (Luke 8:48 KJV)

Pray About His Love

Listen to the words of 1 Peter 5:7 with me; listen with all of your heart: "Give all your worries and cares to God, for he cares about you" (NLT).

What are your "cares" today? Write them below and as you write them, imagine your heart letting go of them and giving them over to the One who sees you, values you, cares about you, and wants to take your burdens upon Himself.

Dear heavenly Father,

I am so humbled that You stop what You're doing and, in the middle of a great crowd, turn to me and grant me healing and wholeness. Your eyes see the whole world and still look upon my life with love, grace, and affection. Thank You for the witness of this woman in today's Bible story. Give me faith like hers, faith that knows You are my only hope. I love You, Lord. In Jesus' name. Amen.

Be About His Love

Something dynamic happens when you remind God of His promises, personalizing them and calling to Him for help. There's no better prescription for deliverance, healing, and victory, especially when you find yourself in the midst of many pressing issues. Just remember as you pray, your love relationship with Jesus is the centerpiece of your life. Give the Lord His rightful place, and everything will fall into focus. Even when your life gets busy today, steal a few minutes to talk with Him.

Look in your favorite study Bible or search online for the promises of God that remind you of your value and your identity as a child of God. Write them on index cards and put them on your mirror, in your wallet, on your dashboard, and other prominent places. Pray these promises and trust that God will be faithful to keep each of His promises to you.

DAY 5: YOU ARE NEVER ALONE

God is our refuge and strength, a very present help in trouble.
Psalm 46:1 NRSV

Think About His Love

When you need God, He is always, always there...there is no appointment required.

I know personally that God relentlessly pursues us, making Himself available when life pulls the rug out from under our feet. I remember one of the most challenging times our family ever experienced. My husband, Charles, suffered a stroke from a blocked artery in his right eye on March 10, 2010. After the diagnosis came the grim prognosis that the stroke had damaged Charles's eye, and he would be totally blind in that eye for the rest of his life.

From the emergency room, Charles was admitted into the hospital and taken straight to the intensive care unit, where he spent an entire week recovering. During the day, our friends and family came by to visit and pray. But I refused to leave Charles's bedside. Each night, I catnapped in the chair alongside his bed, where Charles lay connected to wires and an IV.

I will never forget being on "night watch" in the hospital room. It seems that every dire situation has the potential to be magnified at night. As I sat in his room, reality set in and looked bleaker in the dark hours after midnight. But I can attest to the fact that during those hours I felt God's presence more than any other time I can remember. When our visitors had gone home, Charles and I were kept company by Jesus—the Great Physician, the Great Night Watchman—who never, ever left us.

Don't get me wrong. It was painful to see my husband lying there, hovering between life and death. During those long hours when I cried and prayed, prayed and cried, I found the Lord's presence to be the sweetest of all. And I am glad to report that the doctor's prognosis was wrong. Charles's eyesight began to return after twenty-four hours, and he has no side effects from the stroke!

Charles and I know full well that you don't need an appointment to see Jesus. *He is so good!* Sometimes, a tragedy that comes your way makes you realize just how fragile and priceless life, love, and family can be. They are of inestimable value to us and could never be bought or replaced.

Sweet friend, it's possible that you have dealt with feelings of insignificance at one time or another. More than likely, you have cried many tears during your own long, dark nights. Perhaps you wondered if anyone cared; you might have even pondered if life was worth living. I know you can agree: friends are such a blessing, but they can go with you only so far, especially during times of deep trouble and distress. But praise the Lord, we do not ever have to go the distance alone.

Let Psalm 46:1 encourage you right now, especially if you feel that you are in your darkest hour. This precious promise reminds us: "God is our refuge and strength, a very present help in trouble." God's grace is strongest when you are weak (2 Corinthians 12:9), and He is no respecter of persons (1 Peter 1:17). What Jesus gladly did for me, He will happily do for you.

Jesus understands exactly how you feel. He understands how the world can assault you and leave you standing alone, feeling isolated and vulnerable. He knows what concerns you during the day and what keeps you up late at night. *Jesus understands you better than you understand yourself.*

So, if you have been struggling against the odds, coping with painful issues, don't let anything hold you back. Come back to Jesus. Take refuge in Him; He understands your pain. He is a very present help for you. Whenever you feel down and out, busted and disgusted, let the following words bring this promise back to your mind: *Jesus is touched by how you feel without being subject to sin, so He can touch you at your most vulnerable point and make you whole again.*

Jesus knows how it feels to be unappreciated by those you thought would cheer you on. You see, not only is Jesus the God-Man, the One who put on flesh and came down to earth. He is also the Man-God, the One who is acquainted with our sorrows and carries our grief. When you are hurting, Jesus is broken-hearted too.

I've met so many of you who have shared your hurts with me after concerts, conferences, and retreats. You stood in line, and when it was your turn, you whispered your painful story in my ear. You told me about your lost job and wayward teenager. With tears in your eyes you shared your pain concerning a bad marriage and a bitter divorce. You wore a cute pink ball cap adorned with Austrian crystals, but under it a bald head revealed your relentless fight with cancer. You let me hug your sweet little baby boy who came a few months too soon. You shared that you lost your home due to foreclosure. You rested your head on my shoulder, exhausted from taking care of an elderly mother and two grandchildren who have moved in while their mom was in rehab.

If you feel that life has cheated you out of a relationship or robbed you of your dignity, you are not alone. Look to Jesus as the answer to your problem. If satan has tried to sell you a bill of goods and in exchange steal your joy, dash your hopes, or shatter your dreams, then you are not standing by yourself. Run to Jesus. He is your first choice, not your last resort. He is the ever-present help in trouble.

If you are experiencing tremendous difficulties, let this challenging season motivate you to move closer to God. Let your crisis prompt you to spend intimate time with Jesus.

Too often, we look to others to find our worth and value when we should be looking to Him. Nothing will build you up on the inside like being in the presence of God—the one who calls us *good* and *beautiful*.

Some people seek the applause of others. Some are motivated by a big paycheck, while others are excited by first-class perks. Without Christ, all of these things are empty and meaningless. Jesus is the only One we really need to please. Serve Him as if you were onstage and He was your only audience.

Even at times when you don't seem to feel His presence, it's all right. Don't be led by what you feel. Be led by what you know is true. You are deeply loved by Jesus. Your life is worth more to Him than silver or gold. No matter what circumstances life may bring, look to Jesus to complete you and reveal your true identity. Rest safely in His arms today and soak in the comfort of His presence.

> Don't be led by what you feel. Be led by what you know is true.

Read About His Love

The promise of God's presence is all over the Scriptures.

Read the following Scriptures and write the promise beside each verse.

2 Corinthians 12:9

1 Peter 1:17

Hebrews 4:15

Psalm 16:11

John 14:18

I want to share with you a song I recently wrote about the promise of God's presence, "You Are Not Alone." As you read the lyrics, underline the words that name your situation. Then, circle the words that speak God's sweet promise of presence.

Have you cried a pillow full of tears
Do you pray and then you wonder if God hears
Do you call on friends and loved ones
But find that they're all gone
Well, my friend
You are not alone.

Do you question if it was God's will
And your heart is in a struggle to be still
Are you weak and heavy-laden
On life's long and dusty road
Well, my friend
You are not alone

God is there and nothing is too hard
For His boundless love will meet you where you are
Be of good cheer for He loves you more
Than you could ever know
And my friend
You are not alone*

Pray About His Love

Just as a close friendship or an intimate marriage develops and deepens with time, getting to know Jesus takes time, effort, and commitment. Dear friend, as you draw near to Jesus you are sure to reap great rewards.

Dear sweet Father,
*   I confess that I tend to look to other people to validate me and give me their approval. Forgive me. I need only look to You to experience complete joy and peace.*

Lord, You make life worth living. During those moments when I am alone, help me to steal away to be quiet in Your presence. Lord, help me to understand that I can be alone, but I never have to be lonely. And when I do feel lonesome or in need of company, help me not to feel sorry for myself but, instead, to give You permission to fill my emptiness. In Jesus' name. Amen.

Be About His Love

Jesus said, "I will not leave you comfortless: I will come to you" (John 14:18 KJV). Meditating on God's Word builds strong muscles in our sprit that keep our soul grounded and balanced as we face the issues of life. Today, consider how precious this promise is to you. Say it aloud. Personalize it. Memorize it.

Make a date with the Lord today. Sit outside in a park or another scenic, quiet place. Sit completely alone, in solitude and silence, enjoying His comforting presence. Don't speak. Just listen, enjoy, and be renewed.

VIDEO VIEWER GUIDE

Promise #2: You are _____ to God.

What does it mean to be beautiful in the eyes of God?

1. _____

2. _____

3. _____

God has placed His _____ ____ _____ on your life.

God sees your _____.

When Jesus speaks into our lives, He always speaks _____. He

always _____ _____.

_____ and _____: These two words teach us

more about what it means to be beautiful in the eyes of God.

Week 3

YOU ARE NEVER ALONE

What do you do when facing a difficult situation? Do you share your concern with a family member or friend? Do you cruise the Internet? Though at times these "earthly" options can help, the best place to find life's answers is God's Word. And the only place you can find real love, unexplainable peace, and complete deliverance is in the arms of our loving Lord, Jesus. My dear friend, *He is able*.

This week, we'll continue to explore how Jesus is just as close to you as the mention of His name. Amid the deafening voices of today's culture, you can still hear the voice of God: either as a still, small voice or one that resounds as deeply and widely as the sea. God is calling to you in an unmistakable way—through both His Word and your everyday experiences. As you enter in God's embrace this week, meditate on this: *Because God loves me, He will never leave or abandon me. He recognizes my voice, ever ready to attend to my needs as only He can do.*

Scripture Memorization

Throughout the week, continue focusing on our memory verse, John 17:23 (NCV):

"I will be in them and you will be in me so that they will be completely one. Then the world will know that you sent me and that you loved them just as much as you loved me."

Continue using the index cards in visible places and reading the verse when you get up, throughout the day, and as you go to bed. Remember that another great way to memorize Scripture is to write or type it.

DAY 1: GOD IS NEAR

"Lo, I am with you always, even unto the end of the world."
Matthew 28:20 KJV

Think About His Love

God created you to have sweet fellowship with Him. At the dawn of time, Father God said of Adam, "It is not good that the man should be alone" (Genesis 2:18 KJV). God intended for this first man on earth to enjoy fellowship with Him and with those who would come after him. So, He put Adam to sleep and took Eve out of his side to be his life partner and companion. Then He blessed them together and, at the end of that sixth day of creation, declared that all He had made was "very good" indeed. (See Genesis 1:26-31; 2:18-25.)

There is no question about it. God created us to enjoy good relationships: first with Him and also with others. Connecting with God and our fellow human beings builds us up; it has a very positive effect in our daily lives. I don't know about you, but being with others pours life into me and causes me to thrive.

Many people hunger for connection. This has made social media the power tools of the twenty-first century. Websites, e-mail, and instant and text messaging have allowed us to communicate with family, friends, and business associates all over the world at the click of a button. Yet I have to admit: I have a lot of "old school" in me. When I want to do a quick song demo, I'll sit down at the piano, grab my trusted cassette recorder, and make a replication of my song. Keeping pace with technology is a challenge for me, but I'm doing my best to keep up with millions of people every day who are being connected by cell phones and computers.

In spite of all this progress, however, statistics show that people have never been lonelier and more isolated. Why? Computers can never take the place of enjoying intimate, one-on-one fellowship with God and other people.

My life is richer because of great relationships. But in my often-hurried lifestyle it seems that I have less and less time to invest in them. I'll be the first to admit, when we run ourselves ragged, we sap our physical strength to the degree that it robs us of the joy and meaning Jesus intended for our lives. Finding time to develop and deepen relationships must be one of our greatest priorities in life.

Running at break-neck speed without slowing down to enjoy the relationships God has given you creates the opportunity for the enemy to use your busyness against you. Here's a handy acronym, an old-school tool for your spiritual tool-kit. As you go about your day, never forget...

T oo tired
O verworked
I solated, or
L onely

When we toil, our work is hard and exhausting, and we make slow, difficult progress. I don't want TOIL in my life. Do you? This little acronym is a good reminder for all who are tirelessly trying to keep up in this rat race.

A side effect of toiling is loneliness. When we toil, burning the candle at both ends, we aren't nearly as productive, and often we are very lonely indeed.

Have you ever been in that weary, emotional state of mind brought on by feeling isolated? The sense of separation is very real. People who are alone for long periods of time are extremely vulnerable. Void of real fellowship, they tend to relegate themselves to a lonely existence. When troubles come, they stay in a prolonged state of grief, sadness, and isolation. They may even fight emotional or physical illness longer than their more social counterparts.

In recent years this sense of loneliness and isolation has grown. Most people admit to being lonely at one time or another. Many reveal they have no one with whom they can discuss important or intimate matters. So, more and more people are surfing the Internet these days to satisfy their longing for companionship. What's more, when people are alone and isolated they tend to abuse drugs and alcohol, trying to dull the pangs of loneliness.

Being alone and *being lonely* are two distinctly different things. One can certainly be alone without experiencing loneliness. And one can be truly lonely in a crowded room. Have you ever sensed loneliness and desperation so deeply that you felt numb inside?

If you've ever been lonely, then you know all too well the feeling it brings: a sense that you are alone in the world. There is no deeper hurt than the pain that comes with feeling that you are friendless or that no one cares. Lots of people avoid being lonely by spending more of their time doing too many things. Busyness is one way many well-meaning people try to take their minds off feeling lonely. They tell themselves if they just don't think about it, their loneliness will disappear. But busyness is only a temporary cure. It's like hoping that a toothache will be fixed by avoiding it. Have you ever had a toothache that went away just because you didn't think about it? Of course, not!

We all know such thinking is futile because a toothache always comes back, and it usually seems to get worse at night when you're lying awake trying to make it go away. Oh, yes. Loneliness is very much like this.

Spending money is another way we try to keep lonely feelings at bay. You know how it goes. You tell yourself that if you treat yourself to something new, then you'll feel better. And as it happens with most quick fixes, you actually do feel better for a while,

Being alone and *being lonely* are two distinctly different things.

but inevitably, the pain of loneliness comes back more intense than ever. Depending on how many impulse purchases you've made while shopping, the pain of debt now compounds these lonely pangs.

Spending yourself, that is, giving your heart away, is yet another method we unconsciously use to cope with loneliness. Emotionally, one might determine that a relationship—even with anyone who happens to cross one's path—is all that is needed. Often, these associations are short-lived. Many times, they involve developing unhealthy emotional connections that can lead to casual sex outside marriage.

Let me caution you against giving yourself away like this. When you invest your time, energy, and emotional resources in a relationship that doesn't contribute anything of value to your life, it will always bring you down: leaving you not only feeling lonely, but guilty, ashamed, and filled with regret.

Wherever you are, God is with you. He's keeping you company, journeying with you, holding you in His loving embrace. My hope for you today, dear one, is to know fully that wherever you are, God is already there.

Read About His Love

When Jesus was walking on the earth, He was confined to being one place at a time. But now we have the Holy Spirit, our dear Comforter who is constantly with us—all the time. He lives inside of you and me.

Before Jesus ascended to heaven, He left us a promise. Look in Matthew 28:20 to find that promise. Write it below in your own words.

Reflect on your awareness of God's presence with you. Look around. Where do you see God at work?

Look beyond. Where do you see God drawing you forward?

Look upward. When have you felt God's presence raining down on you?

"Lo, I am with you always, even unto the end of the world." (Matthew 28:20 KJV)

Look inward. How is God at work in you even now?

Memorize Matthew 28:20 and let this truth permeate every moment of every day.

Pray About His Love

As you pray today, filled with faith and resting in God's presence, ask Him to quicken your ears to hear, your eyes to see, and your heart to understand far beyond human limitations what is the height, the depth, and the breadth of God's great love for you.

Dear heavenly Father,

Far too often I'm distracted
Toiling for life's stuff and things
Luring me from my devotion
To You and the peace You bring

Now I see Your plan more clearly
Thank You for a brand new start
Help me follow You more nearly
I love You with all my heart

In Jesus' name I pray. Amen.

Be About His Love

Spend today looking for God. Turn off your computer. Turn down your music. Clear some time from your schedule. Open your eyes to see the ways in which God is moving in every moment of your day and in every relationship. Work on your awareness of God's presence in your life today. Remember, He wants to be actively involved in your day-to-day affairs. Figuratively speaking, open the door of your heart, hang out the welcome sign, and allow Him to make Himself at home there.

DAY 2:
GOD WANTS TO HAVE INTIMATE FELLOWSHIP WITH YOU

May the God and Father of our Lord Jesus Christ be blessed! He is the compassionate Father and God of all comfort.
2 Corinthians 1:3 CEB

Think About His Love

Just as God is the only source of real love, He is the one cure for the pervasive feeling of loneliness. Whenever you feel empty inside, you can have sweet fellowship with Him, for He is "the God of all comfort" (2 Corinthians 1:3 KJV). Over and over in the Bible, we find the Lord reaching out to express His love to His people: revealing Himself to them, pursuing them, longing to fellowship with them, and best of all, communicating intimately with them. First Samuel 12:22 tells us: "The LORD will not forsake his people for his great name's sake: because it hath pleased the LORD to make you his people" (KJV).

I collect coffee table books. My favorites are those filled with scenes of God's beautiful creation. I adore viewing peaceful landscapes of mountains, gorgeous deserts, and expansive prairies. And I love pictures of beautiful beaches. I even enjoy gazing at the casual, bubbling stream that runs behind our house.

Every once in a while I go walking along our country road and bring along my digital camera. My desire is to develop a "photographer's eye." I want to be able to recognize, at a moment's glance, the right subject, the perfect angle, and just the right light to capture one-of-a-kind moments on film, much the way I capture them in a song.

In kind, I can readily admit that if I allow myself to become too busy, I'll miss some sweet moments with God. When an inspired thought comes along, that idea can just as quickly slip away from me if I don't immediately capture it on paper. Likewise, when I'm in songwriting mode, I've even been known to call the voicemail box on our home phone and sing my song ideas into the recorder. I have learned how to avoid letting inspiration get away from me. In the same way, I don't want to get so busy that I miss a beautiful sunrise or sunset, a dazzling shooting star, or a beautiful, fluttering redbird. I want to practice the habit of paying attention to God.

To see God in all of His glory, you don't have to look very far. Just look around. Savor the moment the next time you bite into a vine-ripened tomato, a sweet peach, or a slice of cool watermelon—so sweet that the juice runs down your arm. At that moment, remember to thank God, "who richly provides us with everything for our enjoyment" (1 Timothy 6:17 NIV).

You see, you were born to fellowship with this glorious God who made all the beauty around you. You and I were created and called to enjoy God—to know Him and to make Him known. My sweet sister in faith, you were born to fellowship with God, bring Him pleasure with your life, and put His love on display. It pleases God to call you His own. He desires your intimate companionship and friendship. Because He loves you, He wants you to return His embrace and accept this gift of friendship. He desires you to reciprocate by coming into intimate fellowship with Him.

You can be assured of this: *God's presence will always be with you, even if your closest friends or loved ones abandon you.*

I often think of how Joseph kept his sanity in Pharaoh's prison, how the Apostle Paul endured prison, or how John the Revelator endured being exiled on the island of Patmos. How did Jesus endure the Garden of Gethsemane? I believe—though they had been cut off from friends, betrayed, denied, abused, and accused—each one was fully persuaded he wasn't alone. I am fully persuaded as well. Once you have trusted the Lord Jesus as your Savior, you will never have to be lonely again.

Do you know that Jesus is always with you? Just pause a moment: look around, beyond, upward, inward, and finally in the mirror. Jesus is oh, so near. Christ, the hope of glory, is in you.

Read About His Love

God is always showing off, making sure you know that He is near and right there with you. Just like you did yesterday, I invite you to look beyond, upward, and inward as you study God's Word and pray for open eyes to see His handiwork.

Look beyond. Read Psalm 118:24. How will you be glad in the day that God has set before you?

Look upward. Read Psalm 19:1 and write it below. How are the heavens declaring the glory of God today?

Look inward. Read Colossians 1:27 and write it below. What is your hope in today?

Pray About His Love

Would you pray with me?

This is the day the LORD has made; We will rejoice and be glad in it.
(Psalm 118:24 NKJV)

Dear Father in heaven,

The beauty of Your handiwork comes to mind today. The earth in all its splendor—the endless sky with cotton-candy clouds, the depths of the sea with all its wonderful creatures, the countless stars You call by name, the purple mountains and luscious green valleys: everywhere I look, I see Your majesty on display. You are familiar with it all because You made every inch of it with Your powerful hand. Besides that, You created me because You love me. I am humbled to know that I am fearfully and wonderfully made. So today, I will be more mindful to give You the glory and honor that is due Your name. Absolutely nothing and no one compares to You. It's difficult to find the words to describe Your power. But one word comes to mind. I save this word for You: awesome. Yes, You are an awesome God, and I praise You today. In Jesus's mighty name. Amen.

Be About His Love

Make an effort to rise early one day this week and watch the sun come up on a brand-new day. Sing a song of praise the next time you catch a glimpse of the Big Dipper or the tail of a shooting star trailing across a navy blue night sky. Look in the mirror—a good, long look—and remember that God is pleased to dwell in you and reveal His glory in you.

Pay attention, my dear friend. Don't miss Him. Look for each opportunity to see our heavenly Father in this earthly realm. God, in all of His glory, longs to show how great He is in you.

DAY 3: GOD HEARS

"Call to me and I will answer and reveal to you wondrous secrets that you haven't known."
Jeremiah 33:3 CEB

Think About His Love

At this very moment, God desires to have an ongoing, loving, and life-giving conversation with you.

Imagine you knew that I had a secret to tell you. What would you do? I hope you would respond the way my grandchildren do when I share sweet secrets with them. I have two precious, perfect grandchildren. When they visit, any work that I'm doing is quickly set aside. My personal plans are on hold for another day.

Once when the grandchildren came for a visit, I caught my five-year-old grandson by the arm as he was galloping across the room on his imaginary horse. When I had his attention I said with excitement, "Hey, Punkin!" (That's the name I've given him. I call his big sister, "Precious." She's nine and is cute as a button.)

After getting my grandson's attention, I scooped him up into my arms and held him close. At Grammy's house, casual hugs are not allowed . . . it's all about that lingering embrace: the kind you can feel all the way down to your bones.

I said to him, "Hey, Punkin, I've got a secret! Want to know what it is?" Wide-eyed and excited, he leaned in and placed his ear to my lips. Then he didn't move a muscle. He held his breath, raised his eyebrows, and waited for the "secret beans" I was about to spill. Ever so slowly, I cupped my hand around my mouth. Then with the kind of love, affection, and ridiculous excitement that only a grandmother could muster, I whispered, "You are my only Punkin! I love you."

In return, in that sweet, innocent manner of a five-year-old, Punkin cupped his small, dimpled hand around his mouth and whispered for my ears only, "You're my Grammy! I love you too." Then, he was off and running to slay giants and play with the puppies.

Okay. You can go ahead and stick a fork in me right now because I am done. This grandmother's heart is tenderized by sweet, unconditional love. It just doesn't get any better than that, my friend. Can I say it again? *It just doesn't get any better than that.*

Whenever I read God's wonderful promise in Jeremiah 33:3, I get a vision of the sweet moment I shared that day with my grandson. And it fills my heart with love for God. I sense Him calling to me (wooing me, even) to slow down and listen. He catches me in mid-stride while I'm hurriedly on my way to who knows where, and He compels me to stop, draw nearer, and lean in closer. My precious Father God compels me to hold still and listen intently to what He has to say.

I hold my breath and with great anticipation pay close attention to His words. I surmise that if I, a grandmother, could desire to be so close to and share anything I have on earth with my grandchildren then how much more would God want to share the deepest secrets of His heart and the riches of heaven with me?

As a songwriter, I know that one of the keys to good songwriting is being a good observer. I never know where or how that next song idea is going to reveal itself. The next great song idea, title, first line, or rhyme scheme could be on a billboard alongside the highway or in a magazine ad or a phone conversation or my pastor's sermon. I have to keep my eyes and ears open. *I have to lean in and pay close attention, or I could miss it.*

When my kids were small, being a good mother, I would do everything within my power to supply what my children needed. In the neighborhood where we used to live,

there were 7-Eleven stores on just about every corner. If I needed to dash to the store late at night to get something for one of my children, I could be certain that one of these stores would be open. How much more then does our Father in heaven bless His children from the storehouse of His abundance? I like that comparison. We can go to God 24/7 and receive help in our time of need. He is always open when it concerns being there and providing for us.

A long time ago I heard someone refer to Jeremiah 33:3 as "J-e-r-e-3-3-3" . . . *God's telephone number*. That simple analogy has really stuck with me over the years. Why don't you take a few moments now to commit it to memory too? Guaranteed, you'll need it sooner than you realize. And guaranteed, you'll get through whenever you call.

When the Creator of the universe speaks to you through His Word and says, "Call unto me," He's giving you an open invitation to call Him. Through the miracle of prayer, you can communicate with God—the King and Master of the universe—who loves you deeply. He's never too busy. You don't need to make an appointment, and you won't find it necessary to go through the receptionist in the front lobby. You won't get a busy signal or get put on hold. You won't get any of that when you call on His name. The Lord promises that when you call, He will answer.

Read About His Love

The Bible reminds us over and over again that God hears us when we call.

Read Jeremiah 33:3 and replace the word "you" with your name. Write it in the space below.

Now, read Psalm 17:6. Write a memory of a time that you called upon God and how you experienced God hearing you.

Think about a time that you either gave a child a gift or received a gift as a child. How does it feel to give good gifts to your children? How did it feel to receive good gifts from a loving parent or caregiver?

Read Matthew 7:11 and fill in the blanks.

"Call to me and I will answer and reveal to you wondrous secrets that you haven't known." (Jeremiah 33:3 CEB)

If you who are _____ know how to give _____ _____ to your children, how _____ _____ will your _____ _____ give _____ _____ to those who ask _____.

Underline the promises God makes to His people in Psalm 91:14-16:

Because you are devoted to me,
I'll rescue you.
I'll protect you.
Because you know my name.
Whenever you cry out to me,
I'll answer.
I'll be with you in troubling times.
I'll save you and glorify you.
I'll fill you full with old age.
I'll show you my salvation.

Wow! It just doesn't get any better than that, does it? When God whispers to you, and you cozy up to Him, speaking "sweet somethings" in His ear—His tender mercies begin to overflow in your life. Oh, yes, God definitely hears you when you call on His name!

Pray About His Love

God is ready and waiting to hear from us right now, sweet friend. So let's go to Him in prayer.

Abba, Father, Daddy-God,
You are such an awesome God. I am amazed how You can be everywhere at once, hear the prayers of all Your children, and answer each of us according to our own individual needs! There have even been times when You answered my prayer before I knew I needed what You supplied. Help me not to be anxious. Teach me to rest in the fact that when I call, You will answer—when You want and any way You want. Father, I'll be satisfied because I believe You know what's best for this child of Yours. Thank You, sweet Father. In Jesus' name I pray. Amen.

Be About His Love

Is there something or someone on your heart today? Be about His love by practicing prayer. Present that concern or loved one to the Lord. Throughout the day mention that circumstance or special person by name. Don't worry about it. Instead, with thanksgiving, tell God all about it. In return, His peace will sustain you as you await the answer from Him.

DAY 4: THE FOUR M'S OF PRAYER

Be anxious for nothing, but in everything by prayer and supplication, with thanksgiving, let your requests be made known to God; and the peace of God, which surpasses all understanding, will guard your hearts and minds through Christ Jesus.
Philippians 4:6-7 NKJV

Think About His Love

Today, I want us to take a little time to lean in and look closely at how prayer works. We'll cover four areas, each beginning with the letter m:

The **ministry** of prayer
The **maintenance** of prayer
The **methods** of prayer, and last, but certainly not least . . .
The **miracle** of prayer

The Ministry of Prayer

Once, I was honored to be a guest at Arrendale State Prison in north Georgia. The moment we drove onto the prison grounds and I saw the barbed wire fence encircling the entire property, I began to pray. When we gathered for prayer before the service, I asked God for a special grace to minister to the women. I called upon Him to handpick every inmate who would attend the meeting, to meet the needs of those who would come discouraged, depressed, and filled with doubt, and to give me a concise message to convey His love and hope for His daughters. Then I asked God to help me give a clear invitation for women to receive Christ.

God always gives us more than we ask. Almost eight hundred inmates attended the concert, as well as guards, the warden, and other guests. As I ministered, I observed the singing was louder among those who were incarcerated; it was more joyful and intense. The entire audience was more attentive. There were more *amens* there than in many churches I've visited outside prison walls.

Maybe this is what Paul meant in Romans 5:20 when he said, "Where sin abounded, grace did much more abound." God's spirit moved powerfully in our hearts that night. When the invitation was given, hands went up all over the room to receive Christ as Savior and Lord. Many inmates, though locked in a cell, are freely experiencing God's love and forgiveness today because of the power of prayer.

What a wonderful blessing it is to call unto God! Not only can we receive His love and give Him our love in return; we can cry out to the Lord for others and watch Him move: embracing them with His amazing, unconditional, all-encompassing love.

The Maintenance of Prayer

Just as best friends maintain their relationship by spending time with each other, we maintain intimacy with God through prayer and by reading His Word. Here are some basic keys for you to enjoy a vibrant and productive prayer life.

Adoration. Before telling God all that you need or want, as if you were coming to Him with a shopping list, tell God what He means to you. Tell Him how awesome He is. Recognize His lordship over everything, including your life; then take time to esteem His greatness. This is the perfect time to sing your favorite hymn of praise to God. Regardless of your singing ability, your praises are beautiful to Him.

Confession. Just as keeping your body clean on a daily basis is important, routinely confessing your sins to the Lord is a necessary cleansing exercise for your soul. Nothing can make you feel more alone and isolated from God than sin. So, if you fall into sin, without hesitation run to Jesus with your confession. Your enemy, satan, will tell you to be consumed with guilt and run away from the Lord. But because the price for sin has already been met by Jesus, your sin debt has already been paid! With a grateful heart, you can run to Him for the forgiveness of all your sins. God will hear you and grant your request.

Appreciation. When small children forget that key word at the end of their requests, we prompt them, "Say thank you." This also applies to the children of God when we present our requests to the Lord. The principle of thanksgiving and appreciation is powerful. Thanksgiving is the access code into God's presence, so never forget to say "Thank you" to Him, especially if you have confessed your sins and received forgiveness and cleansing.

Supplication. Tell God what you need. Speak just as you would with a kind and trusted friend, whom you know well and respect deeply. Be honest and transparent as you bring your prayer requests to God. Any good parent wants to bless his or her children, and the Father is pleased to give you the answers to your simplest request or

your deepest need. In the name of Jesus, present all your requests and offerings of prayers to God. As you believe, by faith, you will reap many blessings and avoid countless frustrations.

The Methods of Prayer

Now that you know how to come before God in prayer, how will you know His voice when you hear it? You learn God's voice much the same way you learn to recognize the voices of other significant people in your life. As you spend intimate time with God, you will find it easier to recognize His voice. Here are a few suggestions.

First, read the Bible. Every page contains God's wisdom: His precepts, counsel, and words that speak to the matters of your life. The more you talk to God and read His Word, the more you'll recognize His desire to help you apply His wisdom. The Holy Spirit will help you in this process. There are times when verses will jump off the page as you read them. Other times, you'll hear the Holy Spirit's still, small voice in your heart, bringing a promise to your remembrance.

Second, look to the life of Jesus. Get to know God's only begotten Son. Learn all you can about the life He lived here on earth. Become intimately acquainted with His teachings and His ways. Jesus is the Word of God in flesh. The closer you get to Jesus, the better you hear God's voice.

Third, learn to recognize God's voice through your own experiences. As you draw near to God and follow the Holy Spirit, He will help you see beyond situations in the natural realm. God wants to relate to you right where you are on a very personal level. As you trust Him, walking in obedience to His Word, He will alleviate all your doubts and lead you throughout the day.

I wrote a song with my friend Eddie Carswell called "Trust His Heart." Inspired by the great preacher and author Charles Haddon Spurgeon, we wrote this song quite a few years ago, but the words still ring true: "When you don't understand, when you don't see His plan, when you can't trace His hand, trust His heart."*

The Miracle of Prayer

Years ago, I learned an important lesson concerning what a privilege it is to hear God's voice. I was singing at a music conference that included a very talented young singer by the name of Jaci Velasquez. That day in her concert, she presented her beautiful song, "When I'm on My Knees."

Just before the event concluded, having made our appearances onstage, Jaci and I slipped out into the huge lobby area to get ahead of the crowd and be at our assigned booths at the end of the program. Once the session dismissed, an enormous crowd, somewhere around ten thousand people, streamed into the long, wide halls of the arena.

Jaci's booth was right next to mine. This is when I witnessed something I will never, ever forget. I heard Jaci raise her voice and yell to her father who was way down the corridor, about a hundred feet or so. Trying to gain his attention in the huge crowd, she called out, "Daddy! Daddy!" At that moment, I saw a man in the crowd stop, turn completely around, and look in the direction of her voice. She waved. He caught her eye and waved back to her, acknowledging that he had seen her. Then he shouted back, "Oh! There you are!"

I was stunned. I couldn't believe from so far away, she could recognize him just by seeing the back of his head. I was even more amazed that he could distinguish her voice above all the noises coming from that huge crowd of thousands. And when she called out to him, I saw a simply beautiful thing. She didn't call him some formal name like "Mr. Velasquez" or "Sir." She called him "Daddy." And when she did, no one else turned to answer her voice but him.

This is living proof that every good Daddy knows the voice of his child and delights in answering. It is also proof positive that every child can know his or her Daddy's voice, distinguishing it from any other. What a miracle this is! Do you want to know God like that? I'll tell you, sweet friend, I sure do!

More than anything, God wants to be with you and help you with your decisions. So take Him up on His invitation to bring all your requests before Him. Tell God the deepest secrets of your heart and even more than this, take time to listen to Him. This is when He will reveal the deepest secrets of His heart to you.

Read About His Love

The Bible teaches us so much about how to pray.

Read the following Scriptures and write them below in your own words. Ponder how your prayer life might deepen if you take these words to heart.

1 John 1:9

Psalm 100:4

Psalm 119:10-11

Enter into His gates with thanksgiving, *And* into His courts with praise. Be thankful to Him, and bless His name. (Psalm 100:4 NKJV)

John 16:13a

Philippians 4:6-7

Pray About His Love

Let's put into practice what we've been exploring today! Won't you pray with me?

Dear heavenly Father, Abba, Daddy,
  Thank You for hearing us when we pray. You make Yourself known to us when we need You, and You are a constant presence, even when we're not paying attention. You made amazing wonders for us to know Your power and creativity. You are our great and glorious God. And yet, You are our Daddy. You know our voice when we call from far away. You desire to bless us, hold us, and show us Your love. Help me to release my worries into Your loving care. Teach me to love Your Word and know it well. Give me courage to confess my sin before You and be freed. I will seek You. I will praise You. I will live to lift up Your name. In Jesus' name. Amen.

Be About His Love

Today, meditate on how awesome it is that Father God, the Creator of the universe, gives you an open invitation to call Him. Of the billions of souls living on earth, you have a direct line to talk to the God of the ages! He is never agitated or put off by you in prayer. On the contrary, God welcomes you completely, whether you come to Him with silent cries or shouts of joy. Block out some time today to approach the Lord like a little child, just waiting to hear His secrets. He is attentive to your voice. He responds to your needs. Then, pay attention to God's presence with you all day. How are you experiencing God's answers to your prayers?

DAY 5: GOD WILL MAKE A WAY

Cast your cares on the Lord and he will sustain you; he will never let the righteous fall.
Psalm 55:22 NIV

Think About His Love

God is near to you, and He hears you because He loves you deeply.

The sweet older couple sat across the table from one another, having just finished their dinner in a local cafeteria-style restaurant. Leaving a tip on the table, they situated themselves to leave. With doggie bags wrapped and ready to go, the husband gathered his jacket and ball cap while his dear wife stood to put on her light, all weather car coat. She struggled, wrestling with one sleeve. Her husband came around to her side of the table to assist her. The solution was simple. One of her sleeves had turned inside out, making it impossible for her to find the opening. In no time, the older gentlemen had figured out the problem, straightened the twisted fabric, and helped her into her wrap. Then they were happily on their way.

Isn't that an accurate picture of life? You're faced with a problem that twists and gnarls itself into a knot, so complex you hardly know where it begins and ends. Sometimes life's circumstances can turn everything inside out, leaving you holding a knotted mess of unanswered questions, depleted resources, and strained emotions.

You try this option over here. You wait and hope, hope and wait, only to find that it hasn't worked. So, you try that alternative over there, but after months of treatments and procedures, you find all your efforts futile. As much as you may try, the tangled messes of life are relentless and unforgiving.

Not long ago I visited a friend I hadn't seen in a while. She brought me up-to-date on her journey with pancreatic cancer. The treatments her doctor prescribed had worked temporarily, but the cancer was back with a vengeance and for reasons too numerous to name, surgery wasn't in the picture. The doctor had told her there were no more options. *No more options.*

Some say those words are like a jail sentence. Don't let the jail cell that seems to be erecting itself around you make you lose hope. God holds the key to your deliverance. With Him, there are always options. Trust. Hope. Believe. Stand. God is on your side and He shines best when your situation looks bleakest.

It may seem that everything around you is falling apart and that life is tearing at the seams, but hold on. God cares, and He'll make a way where there seems to be no way. I want to point you to a sister in the Old Testament to remind us that God makes a way. At first, the widow of Zarephath didn't know how much God cared for her. But she would soon discover God had already made a way for her and her family in their time of need.

Come with me to 1 Kings 17 as I continue her story. Help would come to her in the form of a stranger, the prophet Elijah, who had been on the run, fleeing the clutches of King Ahab's wife, Jezebel. These two misguided people were ruling Israel in wickedness. At that time, Ahab and Jezebel worshiped false gods and were leading Israel to do the same. Added to this, Jezebel was seeking to rid Israel of every godly prophet, wanting every last one of them dead.

God holds the key to your deliverance. With Him, there are always options.

Elijah had just declared there would be neither dew nor rain for three years, and as a result there would be a great famine in the land. This was enough to make any Baal worship hot around the collar, since this pagan deity was considered to be the god of the rain.

Elijah had been dwelling by the Brook Cherith, sustained by ravens that brought him fish and bread, morning and evening. He lived by the brook until it dried up. Then God commanded Elijah to go to the city of Zarephath, which was way out of his way and in Jezebel's territory. After he spent many months by the brook and then trekked many days on foot through the dry desert, I can imagine that as Elijah approached Zarephath, he had visions of a warm and tasty home-cooked meal dancing in his head—but alas, God's provision would come in the form of a malnourished widow making plans to cook her last meal.

This fearful woman was probably just as surprised to meet him as he was to meet her. Again, her name is left out of the story. Not a coincidence, right? I admire this widow who encountered a scruffy, tired, thirsty, and hungry stranger at the city gate. Near starvation herself, she had enough compassion on this mysterious stranger to tend to his request. She could have easily left Elijah to fend for himself. She had plenty of reasons to offer any number of excuses. She had a son, another hungry mouth to feed. She was tired and lacked strength. Elijah was a man and a foreigner. She had very few resources. Water was scarce.

As this nameless woman provided food and shelter for the prophet, God took notice of her good deeds. For the next three-and-a-half years, He miraculously cared for her and her son, just as the prophet had said.

This Gentile widow came to know firsthand that there was one true and living God of Israel, and that He knew and cared for her. Widows were more likely than anyone to run out of food during a time of famine, but the great God we serve uses "the foolish things of the world to confound the wise" (1 Corinthians 1:27 KJV): things like flesh-eating ravens to feed a grown man; things such as ordaining a Gentile woman to meet the needs of a Hebrew prophet of God. And just as the Lord had said, this obedient woman's "barrel of meal" did not go empty; neither did her "cruse of oil" fail until the day that the Lord sent rain.

My sister, the promises of God are steadfast and ever true. God cares for you. He's near, He hears, and He'll always find a way for you as you respond in faith to His words.

I heard one young woman testify to this as she shared her "God story" with me. She told me in her letter that one Friday night she'd had all she could take. Fed up, she had determined to take her life. She loaded her gun, got in her car, and headed for the riverbed just a few miles from her apartment.

On the way, she turned on the radio, hoping to hear some music that would drown out her sorrows. The automatic search button on the radio dial stopped on a station; the reception came in loud and clear. It was a station she didn't normally listen to, but she thought, *What difference does it make?* In a few moments, it would all be over anyway. But the music drew her in and arrested her attention. By the time she reached the riverbank the words to the song were sinking in, assuring her that even if it seemed that all hope was gone, God would find a way.

She sat there in her car and listened to the entire song…the words were touching places in her soul that hadn't been touched in a very long time. For the first time since she was a child, the young woman stopped running long enough to receive the precious gift of God's care. Instead of taking her life, she rolled down the window and, with all her might, heaved the handgun into the river.

As it turned out, the song this young lady told me about in her letter was on a live radio program I was doing in her city on that same evening. I was a guest singer for a local Christian radio station that night, and these concerts were always broadcast live over the stations' network. Isn't that powerful? God cares for us so much more than we know.

The song she heard that night, "He'll Find a Way," written by my friend Donna I. Douglas, is a standard in my repertoire, and it contains a timeless message. Only God knew at the very moment I was singing on the other side of town, a young lady would be listening to my concert broadcast on the radio. Her life would be touched, and her mind would be changed, convincing her to give God and life another go.

When life doesn't seem to make sense to you or even seem to be worth living anymore, don't throw in the towel. Let God have the last word on the matter. Don't let satan trick you into thinking that no one cares. God cares for you, my dear friend. And just as He used Elijah, who went far out of his way to reach the starving widow and her family, He will orchestrate all manner of peoples, places, things, and circumstances just to get to you.

Yes, God cares about you. He even cares when you've gotten wrapped up, tied up, and tangled up in the muddled messes of life. He's the only one who is able to rummage through it all and pull out a miracle with your name on it!

Read About His Love

When your situation seems hopeless and you can't see a way out, just look to the stories in the Bible for encouragement.

We find the nameless widow of Zarephath in the book of 1 Kings. Although we do not know her by name, her faith and obedience to God make her stand out. Read 1 Kings 17 and answer the following questions.

When have you felt like you were out of everything—like you only had enough (fill-in-the-blank) to make it through one more moment?

What does this widow's story tell you about God's faithfulness?

Imagine the widow's response to the endless supply of meal and oil. What would you do if you visibly witnessed God's caring provision in your life?

Now, let's rehearse some of the promises of God and write them on our hearts. When you feel like you have no reason to hope, remember these amazing promises from our amazing God. Write them in the space provided and see if you can commit one or more of them to memory.

John 14:18

Philippians 4:19

Zephaniah 3:17

2 Thessalonians 3:3

Isaiah 58:11

Psalm 27:14

Psalm 55:22

Pray About His Love

Are you in need of hope today, my friend? God is our hope. Let's go to Him in prayer.

Dear heavenly Father,

We praise You because You are mighty and You are on our side. If You are for us, who could come against us and prevail? No one. You are invincible. And as mighty, strong, and awesome as You are, God, You care for us so warmly and gently, providing for everything we need to fulfill Your purpose and plan.

Today we cast our cares upon You and we trust You to perfectly care for us. Thank You for stretching forth Your hand against our enemies. Thank You for caring about everything that concerns us. Help us to trust You to fill our days with promise, to establish a godly legacy for our loved ones, to attend to our needs and our broken hearts; and may we overflow with faith and with Your favor. In Jesus' name. Amen.

Cast your cares on the Lord and he will sustain you; he will never let the righteous fall. (Psalm 55:22 NIV)

Be About His Love

Do this exercise now, or wait until later today when you have time to give it your full consideration. Gather two pieces of clean paper. On the first piece, at the top, write this heading: My Cares. On this piece of paper, list your cares and concerns. Make the list as long as you deem necessary. After completing your list, set it aside. Now, at the top of the second piece of paper, write this heading: God Cares. Make a list of all the things you wish to leave in the hands of the Lord. Are your two lists identical? It's okay if they aren't.

Now, read aloud your first list labeled My Cares. Submit it to God. Then as an act of faith, discard or even shred it. Now, pick up the second list labeled God Cares. Read it aloud, and submit it to the Lord, placing all of your concerns in His hands. Then place the list in a location where you can easily refer to it, such as in your Bible.

Don't be anxious about the things you have listed. Remember, you've prayed about and discarded that first list of "anxious cares" before the Lord. I trust that over time, you will continually see His faithfulness. Finally, ask God to help you always remember He is near you, He hears you, and He definitely cares for you.

Today, whenever anxious thoughts try to creep into your heart, be diligent. Guard your heart by declaring today's promise as often as you need it. Be about the Father's love throughout the day by casting your cares upon Him.

Week 3

VIDEO VIEWER GUIDE

Promise #3: You are never _____.

Being _____ and being _____ are two different things.

There is only one person who can _____ what ails us, and that person is

_____ _____.

God wants to have _____ _____ with you.

Ways to practice the presence of God:

1) _____ around and pay attention to _____ _____ with you.

2) Look _____.

Christ _____ _____, the hope of _____.
Colossians 1:27 NRSV

God will _____ you. He _____ for you.

Week 4

YOU HAVE EVERYTHING YOU NEED IN GOD

One of the most reassuring promises God has ever given is that He would provide for us because He loves us. In His perfect knowledge, power, and love, God is able to supply all your needs "according to his riches in glory by Christ Jesus" (Philippians 4:19 KJV).

There will be times when you come face-to-face with very real, obvious needs. But when you know beyond the shadow of a doubt that you are loved by God, you learn from experience that worry is a waste of precious time and energy. You need not worry yourself silly, fretting about how He will provide for you. You must have the assurance, no matter what may come, that He always will.

God has already proved that He is a ready, willing, and able provider. You must decide if you will trust in His provision, even when the things you can see, hear, and feel may not appear to line up with His Word. Remember, don't rely on what you feel. Lean and depend on what you know to be true—the truth of God's Word. This week, I want you to meditate on this promise: *Because God loves me, I have the assurance that He will provide everything I need.*

Scripture Memorization

Throughout the week, continue focusing on our memory verse, John 17:23 (NCV):

"I will be in them and you will be in me so that they will be completely one. Then the world will know that you sent me and that you loved them just as much as you loved me."

Continue using the index cards in visible places and reading the verse when you get up, throughout the day, and as you go to bed. Remember that another great way to memorize Scripture is to write or type it.

DAY 1: GOD IS TRUSTWORTHY

Trust in the LORD with all thine heart; and lean not unto thine own understanding. In all thy ways acknowledge him, and he shall direct thy paths.
Proverbs 3:5-6 KJV

Think About His Love

Father God, the Creator of both the heavenly and the earthly realms, wants you to trust Him with all of your being.

Although I grew up in the state of Michigan, surrounded by an abundance of lakes, rivers, and streams, I never mastered the skill of swimming. Put me on the water, near the water, over the water, or around the water and I'm a happy girl. Put me *in* the water and I'm as happy as a wet hen.

This displeasure goes all the way back to my childhood. When I was in junior high school, swimming class was a required course. I dreaded every moment of that six-week marking period. Though I did the best I could, I never felt confident enough to venture into water that was over my head. For me, the entire course was spent in the shallow end of the pool. Our physical education teacher was patient with me, offering constant encouragement from the pool deck; and she made sure that I didn't lose sight of the challenge that was out in front of me. For six weeks I did the best I could to learn the basics of swimming. On the dreaded day when I was required to swim the entire length of the pool, I made certain that I swam near the edge where I could reach out and grab hold of the side in case I needed to stop and catch my breath or wipe the stinging chlorinated water from my eyes. By the grace of God and the mercy of my teacher, I passed the course.

I'm not sure why this swimming thing never really caught on with me. It could have been because I didn't like getting my hair wet or putting my face in the water. The chlorinated water stung when it got into my eyes, ears, and nose. Maybe, as a self-conscious seventh grader, I was embarrassed and self-conscious in that faded blue, ill-fitting, public-school-issued swimsuit we all had to wear. Maybe I didn't trust my ability to navigate the deep water when it really mattered. I'm sure all of that played a part in my inability to acclimate to the deep end. One thing was certain: I felt like a fish out of water. I felt awkward, ugly, uncertain, and clumsy. I wanted to be in a position where I could manage my situation—to get to an environment where I could feel in control.

Many Christians are like that. They are casually acquainted with God and even know a little bit about Him. They go to church and may even attend Bible study or other church activities. They enjoy singing in the choir or volunteering to work in the nursery. But they never venture into the "deep end"—into a trust-God-with-all-your-heart type of relationship. They are comfortable with walking along the water's edge of religion where their feet barely get wet.

Could that be you, my friend? Has your relationship with God been safe and predictable? Do you long to understand more fully what it means to trust God with a fall-backward, blind-folded kind of faith? Do you need to know for sure that God will catch you—that He has your back when life's overwhelming circumstances arise and situations are over your head?

Staying afloat in life can be a real challenge. Right now you may feel like you're going under for the third time. Maybe you trusted people but they disappointed you. Does any of that sound familiar? I've got good news for you! Jesus is trustworthy! He is the hope you have been searching for. He is a strong but gentle Friend, subduing angry waves and navigating life's storms. He loves you, and He is here for you. You can trust Him completely and confidently.

Today, I want you to know the powerful promise in Proverbs 3:5-6. To trust in the Lord with all your heart means to set all your hopes upon Him: to possess a bold confidence and a sure security in God, fearing nothing. It is having complete and total confidence in the Lord, resting in Him instead of in our own thoughts, the opinions of others, or in our circumstances. It is in the Lord, and in Him alone, that we can fully trust. His ways are tried and true.

To trust Jesus the way the Father desires, it is essential for you to maintain an intimate, ongoing relationship with Him. People don't usually trust strangers or casual acquaintances they don't know very well. And this is wise because trust is never established casually. It's earned over time, by spending countless moments together, sharing one's confidences and concerns.

When I was in that swim class in seventh grade, every once in a while I would lean back in the pool and let the water carry me. I'd float and relax, allowing the water to hold me up. In the same way, you can enjoy a relationship of confidence and complete trust in the Lord by spending time in His presence—so much so that when challenges come, you are able to let go of every fear and concern and rest in His loving arms. As you experience God's unfailing presence in your life, you will find that to know Him is to love and trust Him more and more and more.

When you really trust God, you can truly let go of any and all worry and concern. When everyone else drops the ball concerning your situation, the Lord proves He is worthy of your trust. He never changes. His very nature doesn't permit Him to fail. Our heavenly Father is not like shifting shadows, unstable winds, or changing tides. You can trust Him completely with all that you are and with everything you possess. You can trust Him with all your heart, giving yourself to Him fully, freely, and without hesitation.

To trust Jesus the way the Father desires, it is essential for you to maintain an intimate, ongoing relationship with Him.

Read About His Love

No matter what situation you face, you can trust that you are safe in God's arms.

Are you a good swimmer, or are you uncomfortable in the deep end of the swimming pool? What does the pool represent in your life today? What situations come to mind that seem like an exercise in trust? Draw a swimming pool and write your fears and doubts in it.

Every good and perfect gift is from above, coming down from the Father of the heavenly lights, who does not change like shifting shadows. (James 1:17 NIV)

Read Proverbs 3:5-6 in a few different translations of the Bible. Envision yourself jumping with confidence into the deep end of the swimming pool. How can you trust God and jump headlong into the safety of God's outstretched arms? What would this mean for you?

James 1:17 tells us something about the nature of God's trustworthiness. How does this verse prove God's trustworthiness to you?

In Jeremiah 1, God called a young boy named Jeremiah to become His prophet to Israel and to the nations. Father God made him a promise in verse 12. What does this promise tell us about trusting God's Word?

Likewise, Jesus left us with a promise in Matthew 24:35 that points to the trustworthy nature of God. What is that promise?

Pray About His Love

God is always trustworthy! Let's turn to Him now in prayer.

My dear Father,

You are faithful and true. There is no compromise or shadow of turning in You. I praise You that when everything around me is shifting, You remain constant. When I am faced with questions I cannot answer, I can look to Your wisdom. When I am challenged and find life extremely difficult, I will turn to You for strength and direction. You have already proved that You will remain steadfast and trustworthy. Forgive me for withholding my trust from You when others betrayed me, for You are my refuge and my shelter. All my hope and trust are in You. When I encounter situations that seem to be over my head, I know You will not allow me to be overwhelmed. Instead, like the perfect Father You are, You will catch me, even if it feels like I'm going under the waves of trouble. I love You, Lord. In Jesus' name I pray. Amen.

Be About His Love

Imagine that you are a student with me in my seventh grade swim class. Picture my struggle and hesitation to venture into the deep end of the swimming pool. Now look back at the swimming pool of fears and doubts that you drew previously. In which areas of your life have you hesitated most in trusting God? Which ones have created negative cycles in your life that you'd like to overcome?

Present these areas to God. Surrender them to Him completely. Then close your eyes and picture yourself gliding effortlessly, like a well-trained Olympic swimmer, through the water in the deep end of the swimming pool. Yes, the water may be way over your head, but it's okay because you have complete peace as you navigate the deep. In the same way, bask in the confidence of putting complete trust in your Heavenly Father as if your very life depended on it. And you know what? It does!

Let me encourage you to pray wholeheartedly about any area in your life that seems to be way over your head. God is at work today. He will give you wisdom and help you come back up to the surface in each area, completely safe—ready to take the plunge again.

DAY 2: GOD'S WISDOM IS PERFECT

All God's words are tried and true; a shield for those who take refuge in him.
Proverbs 30:5 CEB

Think About His Love

God is all-knowing. He understands everything there is to know about time and space because He created them. He knows about the past, the present, and the future—because He lives in the eternal realm outside the sphere of time and seasons. Our heavenly Father has complete knowledge and understanding about people, as well as powers in the spiritual realm. He created it all. His understanding is perfect.

The Bible calls God omniscient. Simply defined: He knows everything. We could study a subject for years, earn a degree, and even teach it for a period of time; still, our knowledge of that subject matter might be minimal at best. First Corinthians explains that "we know *in part,* and we prophesy *in part.* But when that which is perfect is come, then that which is *in part* shall be done away" (13:9-10 KJV, emphasis mine). As long as we are wrapped in human flesh, living in this world, we simply cannot know everything.

But God does. Yes, God knows everything, and He especially knows about you. When God created the heavens and the earth, He said, "Let there be . . ." and it was so. Then on the sixth day He created the first man: Adam. He didn't just say, "Let us make man in our image . . ." He stooped down, gathered up some dust, and then blew His very nature into him. (See Genesis 1:6-10, 26-27, 2:7.)

So you see, innately, in the deepest part of your being, you have the capacity to have deep communion with God. You possess the ability to trust the wisdom of God without hesitation—because part of you comes from the earthly realm, and the other part is divine.

God has a vast understanding of every intricate detail of your life. His wisdom concerning you is without limitation and beyond comparison because He made you. He knows you completely: inside and out. He also knows that as you spend time with Him, both in His Word and in prayer, you will look at the circumstances of life—even those things that may appear to be harmful to you—and say, "I'm safe in my Father's arms."

Because He is all-knowing, God is already aware of any sinful thoughts or attitudes you may want to hide. He knows the earthly part of you that He formed from the dust. He knows that your sin will make you want to run away from Him. That's why, when you're looking into the deep abyss of your sins, afraid of drowning because of your own inabilities, He has mercy on you. He keeps calling you to come to Him, again, and again.

Hear me now: If your relationship with God is breached for any reason, He didn't cause it. But if your relationship is to be restored, you must respond in faith to Him.

Not only is God all-knowing but He is all-wise. He will never misconstrue the intents of your heart. He is not like people who tend to misunderstand or confuse what you say with what you really mean. There are no secrets within you that can surprise God, causing Him to say, "Wow, I wish you hadn't told me *that.* If I had been aware of *that,* I would have had nothing to do with you!"

Rest assured, my friend. God already knows everything about you. He understands every detail about your strengths and weaknesses; He is intimately acquainted with your hopes, dreams, and desires. After all, He created you and placed them inside you. God already knows the end from the beginning in every area of your life. You can rely on His perfect wisdom. And as His Word promises, "He shall direct your paths" (Proverbs 3:6 NKJV).

God's wisdom is inconceivable, unsearchable, and uncontainable. He is trustworthy, all-knowing, and all-wise. Not so for humanity. Even when our motives and intentions are right, we cannot place our full trust in human flesh: not in other people, not even in ourselves. On our best day, our most profound ideas, agendas, and plans are limited. For example, many entrepreneurs and company CEOs have proved that humanity's ideas and systems, at one time or another, have failed. Even the most creative and insightful ideas have to go back to the drawing board at times.

It is said that around the year 1896, Henry Ford failed to put a reverse gear in his first automobile. He also failed to put a garage door in the shed where the automobile was built. The result? He had to demolish the shed to get the car out.[1]

In recent years financial systems all over the world have failed millions of people, resulting in bank failures, the crashing of the stock market, the collapse of the real estate market, and a crumbling economy. Humanity's systems will always fail because they are temporal and earthly . . . made by human beings.

Anything you can see with your natural eyes is temporary. If you can see something, one day it will decay and fade away. Houses, cars, money, clothes, products—none of them will last. Each will ultimately crumble and fall.

God's systems are eternal. Like His Word, they will stand forever. Because you can always trust God's Word, you can be stable, trusting His (not humanity's) economy and knowing His plans (not humanity's) will stand the test of time.

My dear friend, you can rely on God's pure, holy, and powerful word! It will never pass away. He knows everything there is to know about everything. God's wisdom is perfect, and because this is so, you can always trust that *His kingdom* (not the kingdoms of human beings) will last forever. *His will* (not the plans and purposes of people) will be accomplished in the earth for His glory. Let 2 Corinthians 4:18 encourage you: "We look not at the things which are seen, but at the things which are not seen: for the things which are seen are temporal; but the things which are not seen are eternal" (KJV).

God's wisdom is perfect because He sees the past, present, and future. He knows exactly what we need before we need it—He is just so good to provide our every need. Because God loves you, He will show you His wisdom and clear a path for you to find your way. You can avoid confusion and mistakes every time by asking for and following His direction.

Trusting God doesn't mean you don't ask questions. Sometimes life bombards you with things that just don't make sense. For some, it's easy to point a finger at God when they consider life's most difficult questions. Over the years, I have heard from many people who pour out their hearts in a card, letter, or e-mail that comes across my desk. My heart breaks as I consider what they ask:

> We look not at the things which are seen, but at the things which are not seen: for the things which are seen are temporal; but the things which are not seen are eternal.
> (2 Corinthians 4:18 KJV)

"Why do bad things happen to good people?"

"Why would God allow over 2,900 victims to perish in the attacks on the Twin Towers on September 11, 2001?"

"Why would God allow innocent children to be sold into the sex trade?"

"Why did my friend's husband die of cancer, leaving her to put two children through college on a teacher's salary?"

"When will my grown children give their lives to the Lord?"

"When will my husband find a good job?"

What about you? Do too many questions and not enough answers leave you reeling and wondering most days? Do they cause you to lie awake many nights, pondering whether things will ever work out? As you wade through all the questions in your life, let me offer a word of hope. No matter how tough your life may be—no matter how bleak things may look or how difficult your situation may get—you can always hold fast to the hope that God is perfectly reliable and dependable and His wisdom is perfect. He is bigger than any question you may face, and He can handle any question you may have. Facing changes? Changes may surprise you, but nothing takes God by surprise. Got issues? Just like Jesus healed the woman with the issue of blood, He is able to heal the issues in your life. Got problems? No problem. Jesus is the problem-solver. Turn your problems over to Jesus.

You may never know the answer to some of life's questions on this side of heaven. When you encounter life's difficult questions, consider this: Instead of asking *why,* ask *how*. Ask God how He might change your heart so that He can receive glory from the struggles in your life. Ask your Father how He might use you to help someone who is going through a similar struggle. Trust your Heavenly Father to sustain you so that as you *go through* a situation you can grow through the situation. Without fail, He loves you without condition. Without fail, without exception, you can trust Him. So, come boldly before His throne of grace. Ask for His wisdom. The Bible promises He'll give it to you freely and liberally.

Read About His Love

God's Word has been tried, tested, and proved true throughout history. The wisdom and truth in the Scriptures lead us to trust in God's wisdom.

Read the following Scripture passages and look for recurring themes: 2 Samuel 22:31-33; Psalm 11:7-8; Proverbs 30:5. What do these verses tell us about God's wisdom?

Why do we worry so? Why do we waste our time, energy, and emotions on things that we have no control over? Worry is nothing new. Jesus had to remind the crowds not to worry. Read Matthew 6:31-34. Then circle all the things below that you can add to your life by worrying.

peace
joy
hope
suffering
despair
confusion
burnout
fatigue

Ladies, hear me today. God is all-knowing, all-loving, and so very trustworthy. He is all wisdom and has every answer for every problem you will ever face. Trust His loving hand to guide you, seek His perfect wisdom, and feel the warm embrace of the great God who calls you His own.

Pray About His Love

I want to encourage you with another simple prayer that I wrote for this week's study. Would you pray these words with me today?

Dear gracious, heavenly Father,

Too often when I face life's trials
Problems seem over my head
I feel like I am going under
Overwhelmed with waves of dread

I know you know what's best for me
When I don't see or understand

> Every word of God is pure; He is a shield to those who put their trust in Him. (Proverbs 30:5 NKJV)

You are too wise to be mistaken
You hold my future in Your hand

So I confess, You are the answer
You are faithful, tried, and true
I will trust in You completely
To lead me, guide me safely through

This is my sincere prayer to You today.
In Jesus' name. Amen.

Be About His Love

Today, as you go about your regular work and play, be aware of how many times you worry about this or that. When you feel yourself worrying, write down your cares on a slip of paper. Remember that God knows your situation and knows exactly how to lead you to victory. Once you have written down your worries, wad them up and toss them in the trash. Remember that you cannot add one good thing to your life by worrying. Instead of worrying, train yourself to pray and rest in the assurance that God knows how to give good gifts to His children.

DAY 3: GOD GIVES COURAGE

Have not I commanded thee? Be strong and of a good courage; be not afraid, neither be thou dismayed: for the LORD thy God is with thee whithersoever thou goest.
Joshua 1:9 KJV

Think About His Love

God has given you courage to go to battle in His name, knowing He has already provided everything you need for a sure victory. Today and tomorrow, we'll look at the aspects of a life of courageous faith as we study the story of Joshua.

> God knows your situation and knows exactly how to lead you to victory.

God chose Joshua to be the leader of the Israelite nation after forty years of wandering in the desert just before Moses' death (see Deuteronomy 31:7-8, 23). Under the Lord's direction, Joshua would take God's people into a great, new land—the promised land. To carry out God's plan, they would have to conquer the inhabitants of this land of promise: Canaan. That meant, first of all, overtaking the great and mighty city of Jericho. When Joshua received his instructions, God assured Him of His protection and guidance. He told Joshua to "Be strong and of good courage . . . for the LORD your God is with you wherever you go" (Joshua 1:9 NKJV).

What a powerful promise! Joshua needed to hear and embrace every word of it because the city of Jericho was a mighty fortress. Surrounded by massive walls, it had an insurmountable defensive structure encased on every side. At first glance, I'm sure it seemed impossible to penetrate. But Joshua knew that this walled fortress stood between the Israelites and God's will for the nations: to enter and possess Canaan, the promised land.

In this unforgettable story, God instructs Joshua and the Israelites to do nothing for the first six (of seven) days, except to march around the city of Jericho once a day. No talking back or complaining would be allowed. As a matter of fact, Joshua instructed them that no one could open his mouth. Along with this, he told them not to fear. He warned them not to fight. He specifically instructed them not to do anything except to march, in the exact order and way he described.

I can see this scene unfolding in my mind's eye as the people of Israel walked and walked around the walls of Jericho. No doubt, on day one, their enemies laughed at them as they paced around the city. On day two, after laughing came the mocking, but God's people kept on walking. On day three, I can just hear the Canaanites taunting the people of God, heckling them from atop the city wall. This was a true test of courage for the children of Israel. I can imagine they probably felt intimidated. But they continued to walk all the same.

Has God ever held you in a holding pattern, waiting for His next command? I fly a lot. Often, I travel many miles across this country, as well as in foreign lands, singing and speaking. I'm happiest when my flights are predictable. I want every flight to leave right on time. I want my pretzels and my spicy tomato juice with no ice and a wedge of lime at the expected moment midflight. Then I want to read a couple of chapters from a good book and take a short nap just before landing.

But every once in a while, for one reason or another, the plane I'm traveling on has to go into a holding pattern. I don't like holding patterns. They tend to make me nervous. I feel as if my fellow passengers and I are in the middle of nowhere, going around and around in endless circles. Besides this, a holding pattern usually means a delay. I don't like delays either. I've missed flight connections because of delays. I've been late getting to a few concert engagements because of delays.

But I realize that when I'm in those situations I can't see the big picture. From my perspective, I can't see all the things that have caused the delay. As my flight waits in a holding pattern, air traffic control communicates with the pilots in every plane that is affected. Then at just the right time in the "big picture" schedule, the pilot of the aircraft I'm on receives the instructions to come out of the holding pattern. I heave a sigh of relief as we prepare to land.

People haven't changed. We don't like waiting today any more than the people of Israel did as they were walking continuously around the city of Jericho. We get impatient for the popcorn to finish popping in the microwave oven. We grow weary waiting in line at the fast food drive-thru. And we certainly have a tendency to get impatient when we're waiting on God to fix our personal situations, don't we?

We want God to move speedily. We don't like it when He makes us wait.

But aren't you glad that God knows best? Doesn't it give you a great sense of peace in your heart, just knowing that God is in complete control . . . even while, on the surface, a situation appears to be exactly the opposite? At face value, there are many times you may feel that God is far off, maybe even aloof and uncaring, about your situation. Don't fall for that trick of the enemy, dear one. The devil will try to convince you every time that God doesn't care about you or your problems. The father of lies would have you believe that God is too busy to look your way. Your adversary keeps telling you all the time to throw up your hands and quit. But don't even go there, my friend!

The devil is a hater. But God loves you. The devil is a discourager, and he wants to bring you down. God is an encourager, and He will lift you up.

God is working. God is moving. There are moments in our lives when we just have to give Him time. Behind the scenes, God is using what looks like chaos at first glance and sounds like absolute mayhem. But in His great power, He is turning things around. He is creating a beautifully orchestrated symphony, aligning all things in perfect harmony to work *for your good and for His glory*.

Until the right moment reveals itself, God expects you to be humbly obedient to His Word. Don't talk back. Don't complain. Don't make a sound of defiance. Does this remind you of anything? No matter how high the wall may be; no matter how many times God tells you to encircle it; regardless of anything the enemy is screaming at you, *don't fear, don't struggle*, and definitely *don't fight*. Keep your heart fixed upon the Lord and obey Him. *Just keep marching.*

As you obey God's marching commands, keep trusting in His great love for you. It takes tremendous courage to keep marching on when you're uncertain how your situation is going to turn out. It takes bold, audacious faith in God to keep moving forward on His instructions, even when you feel He is keeping you in the dark.

My friend, if this is where you are right now, do what the Israelites did: keep marching, no matter what. In return for their faith and trust in Him, God granted them a sure victory. In fact, He has a great victory waiting for you! God will perform His word for *your good and His glory*—but He will do it in His own time.

Read About His Love

When you face life's trials and feel like defeat is imminent, remember Joshua and take courage. God will show up and do a mighty work in His own time.

Read Joshua 1:6-9. How many times do you find the words courage or courageous in this passage?

Where does Joshua's courage come from?

In verse 9, God reminds Joshua that having courage isn't a suggestion but a command. What situations in your life require courage on your part?

Say aloud Joshua 1:9, letting each word sink deeply in your heart:

"Have I not commanded you? Be strong and courageous. Do not be afraid; do not be discouraged, for the LORD your God will be with you wherever you go." **(NIV)**

As you meditate on this verse today, put yourself in Joshua's place. What has God commanded you to do?

Psalm 27:1-4 (CEB) is a declaration of taking courage in God. Underline the words that give you courage that God will see you through your trials.

The LORD is my light and my salvation.
  Should I fear anyone?
The LORD is a fortress
  protecting my life.
  Should I be frightened of anything?
When evildoers come at me
  Trying to eat me up—
  it's they, my foes and my enemies,

who stumble and fall!
If an army camps against me
my heart won't be afraid.
If war comes up against me,
I will continue to trust in this:
I have asked one thing
from the LORD—
it's all I seek—
to live in the LORD's house
all the days of my life,
seeing the LORD's beauty
and constantly adoring his temple.

Pray About His Love

Would you pray with me?

Almighty God,

Some days I feel as if I'm fighting a losing battle, taking two steps forward and three steps back. And when I look at things with my natural eyes, it seems that every-thing in my world is falling apart. My life is full of speed bumps, potholes, detours, and delays, Lord. Sometimes my bill box is nearly full and my gas tank is nearly empty. If I didn't know any better during these tests of my faith, I'd think the whole world was turning against me. But I praise You that I do know better! I know that if You are for me, You are much greater than whatever is coming against me. So today, sweet Father, I ask for courage to do what You require of me in any situation and es-pecially when I feel like I'm in a holding pattern. Thank You for the victory that is already mine in Christ Jesus, in whose name I pray. Amen.

Be About His Love

Embrace the tangible presence of God's love in your life today. Remember that some battles are fought and won with weapons; others are fought and won with praise! Be about His love by obeying God and letting Him defeat the enemy on your behalf. Amen!

Day 4: God Gives Confidence

"I will not leave you comfortless: I will come to you."
John 14:18 KJV

Think About His Love

So keep at your work, this faith and love rooted in Christ, exactly as I set it out for you.
2 Timothy 1:13 *THE MESSAGE*

Think About His Love

Friends, today I want to continue a little further into Joshua's story to discover his confidence in and commitment to God's plan.

Remember that the Israelites were to march around the Jericho city wall without complaining or groaning for six days. On the seventh day, the children of Israel marched around the city seven consecutive times. Joshua instructed the priests to blow their trumpets and told all the people to lift up a shout of victory at the appointed time. When the trumpets blew and the people shouted, the walls of Jericho came tumbling down (Joshua 6:20).

God's ways truly amaze me! Not only does He move *when He wants*. He moves *how He wants*. Maybe Joshua's way to tackle that situation would have been to scale the wall or sneak through a crack or crevice somehow. But Joshua knew God. He trusted God's wisdom, knowing the results would be better in the end. From walking many years alongside Moses, he knew all too well that God has His own way of doing things. In Isaiah 55:9, our heavenly Father declares: "For as the heavens are higher than the earth, so are my ways higher than your ways, and my thoughts than your thoughts" (NKJV).

To stay in step with God's plan, the people of Israel had to go through the repetitious exercise of circling the city once a day for six days. That way, on the seventh day, when they had to circle it seven times, they were warmed up for it: spiritually, physically, emotionally, and otherwise. Besides that, the number six is often interpreted as being the number of humankind, and seven is generally understood as being the number of perfection and divine completion. I guess you could say God allowed the Israelites to come to the end of themselves before He stepped in to complete and perfect the process by doing what only He could do. Have you ever had a "Jericho experience"? I've had a few of them.

I often wonder why God does things the way He does them. For example, why would God permit the children of Israel to wander around in the desert for forty years when the journey to the Promised Land should have taken only a fraction of the time?

On your journey through life, have you ever wondered why you sometimes have to go over rough mountains and through deep valleys? Have you ever gone through dry spells and tight spots? Do you sometimes encounter delays and detours? Take heart, my friend, *God is working*.

When God led the Israelites out of Egypt, they wandered for forty years before they got to this scene with Joshua and the wall of Jericho. And you know what I've discovered? The people didn't get lost in the wilderness; that was God's plan for them to take the long way. God created this divine detour. He ordained their delay.

In His infinite wisdom, God always knows what is best for His people. Had He taken them to Canaan by the most direct route, they would have encountered the Philistines sooner than they were prepared to do so. The Philistines would have caused the first generation of Israelites that left Egypt to become paralyzed with fear. God knows that when we are fearful, we run. The Israelites would have run right back to Egypt, back to captivity and the cruel yoke of slavery.

Running back to slavery would have meant going back into bondage, which would have meant going back into a life of oppression. And once living in oppression, the Israelites would have gone back into suppression. Suppression would have eventually landed them in the middle of living lives of depression—which is where their parents were when God sent Moses to deliver the nation out of the hands of the enemies. Oh, no! God wasn't going to allow that to happen!

Listen, my friend. If you are experiencing one of life's delays or detours on your journey, it doesn't mean that God has forgotten about you. On the contrary, God loves you. You are constantly in His heart and mind. God could never forget about you. He is well aware of your situation.

If you are on a detour right now, it is the true test of your confidence in the Lord. From His vantage point of knowing all and seeing all, you must be confident that His thoughts are higher than yours and that He knows your end from your beginning. Trust God with all of your heart, and don't lean unto your own understanding. He is a faithful provider every step of the way.

Charles and I have discovered that sometimes God takes us through a situation because He knows it will make us stronger and eventually better. But at other times He gently leads us on a detour around a situation. Remember this: what may appear to be a delay or a detour doesn't necessarily mean denial. God is on our side; He is preparing us for the future and protecting us from harm.

As the people of God walked around Jericho's walls for seven days straight, they were committed to one single cause—taking the city. In order to be victorious, they had no choice but to do everything God's way. Resorting to any other plan would have meant certain destruction.

For whatever reason, the Lord had given Joshua and the army of Israel very specific instructions about who went first, and what each group did as they marched. Focused on God to achieve their purpose, the people humbly obeyed the Lord, following every command. They were unwaveringly committed to God's plan because they needed God's results.

So never pull back when God requires strict compliance from you in any area of your life. Because it usually means He's setting you up for a perfect, highly uncommon result. In any and all endeavors, if you want to experience the level of success God desires for you, be unwaveringly committed: both to Him and to thoroughly executing each step of His plan. Remember, God has already given you the innate ability to rise to the occasion.

The famous battle at Jericho will always be the subject of Sunday school lessons around the world, but to the seasoned believer who wishes to do God's will, this inspiring story is much, much more. For here we find a man who is totally sold out to God and His cause. We see someone who is completely willing to lay down his life and put the lives of an entire nation in jeopardy, all because he had confidence in God and was committed to God's plan.

No matter what you're facing, there is always hope in God. So, be courageous. Have confidence in Him. Remember that hope is not wishing on a star, crossing your fingers, taking a chance, or stepping out on a "wing and a prayer." Hope is confident expectation of good. It is the anticipation that God will work everything out. Hope says, "It may not be okay right now. But it's going to be all right." Stand firm in your faith, boldly committed to the Lord. He will faithfully provide for all your needs as you obediently trust Him in every situation.

> Hope is the confident expectation of good. It is the anticipation that God will work everything out.

Read About His Love

We can have confidence in knowing that God is for us and working for our good.

Read Exodus 13:17-22. Why did God take the Israelites the long way?

How did God provide direction?

When you are totally committed to a God-ordained endeavor, success is certain. Listen to the words of the Apostle Paul, writing to Timothy, his son in the faith and a firmly committed disciple of Jesus Christ:

This is the Message I've been set apart to proclaim as a preacher, emissary, and teacher. It's also the cause of all the trouble I'm in. But I have no regrets. I couldn't be more sure of my ground—the One I've trusted in can take care of what he's trusted me to do right to the end. So keep at your work, this faith and love rooted in Christ, exactly as I set it out for you. It's as sound as the day you first heard it from me. Guard this precious thing placed in your custody by the Holy Spirit who works in us.

2 Timothy 1:11-14 *THE MESSAGE*

What has God trusted you to do?

What does it mean for you to "keep at your work"?

What does it look like for you to be confident in the promises of God?

American racecar driver Mario Andretti once said, "Desire is the key to motivation, but it is determination and commitment to an unrelenting pursuit of your goal—a commitment to excellence—that will enable you to attain the success you seek."[2] God demonstrated His eternal commitment to excellence during the Battle of Jericho. Every element had to be perfectly in place, and timing was critical. You see, God had a supernaturally perfect result in mind—tons of stone broken down and crushed together around a once formidable enemy encampment—without His people raising one hand to make it happen.

What is the "wall" that you are marching around right now? What is the goal you are pursuing?

Take heart, my friend. Be courageous, confident, and committed to the work that God is doing and will do in your life.

Pray About His Love

Won't you pray with me?

Father God,

Today we pray for confidence that You will do what you say You will do. I ask for confidence to carry out Your instructions, even when my mind can't make sense of them. And, Lord, I ask for a heart that is singularly committed to Your cause. I realize this is a dangerous request because asking this of You potentially invites more drama into my life. But I know that when I am weak, You are strong. And depending on Your strength is where I want to be. I know it's just a matter of time until I cross over into Your promised land of victory in my life. I love You, Lord. In the name of Your Son, Jesus, I pray. Amen.

Be About His Love

Can you envision your promised land while staring directly at the walls of *your* Jericho? As your life intersects with God's love today, ponder the battles that God has already won in your life. Now, see yourself victorious as you obey God's new and unique battle plan.

Pray about the things God has instructed you to do for His kingdom and glory. If personal struggles have kept you from fulfilling one, a few, or all of them, it's time to run to the Father and receive grace and mercy in your time of need. Remember, the presence of hardship in your life does not mean that God's love is absent or that He won't help you defeat the enemy. As you go through your day, actively listen for and commit to God's instructions. Follow Him where he leads and praise Him along the way, "for His mercy endures forever!" (Psalm 136:1 NKJV).

DAY 5: REST IN GOD

"Come unto me, all ye that labour and are heavy laden, and I will give you rest. Take my yoke upon you, and learn of me; for I am meek and lowly in heart: and ye shall find rest unto your souls. For my yoke is easy, and my burden is light."
Matthew 11:28-30 KJV

Think About His Love

Father God wants you to understand, relish, and rest in the fact that Jesus is your supply. Our loving Lord provides everything you need according to His riches in glory.

Do you know someone who is constantly on the run? From the moment she puts her feet on the floor at the crack of "dark-thirty" to the moment she lays her head down well after midnight, she's on the run. She runs to work, to school, to the bank, to the cleaners, to the baseball field, and to church. And of course, she runs behind. She runs late. She runs out. She runs scared. The chaos hardly ever ceases. Even when she should be asleep, she lies awake with a long list of things to do and places to go running through her head. Now, she's running short on sleep! There is no rest for the weary, is there?

Ah, but there is, my friend. Jesus extends a personal invitation for you to step out of your position in the fast lane. He invites you to get off the endless treadmill of life. He invites you to wipe the sweat from your brow, exhale the breath you've been holding, and sit down to rest. Take a breather. You know you need it. Rested people are healthier, refreshed. They look better and are more fun to be with.

Jesus knows how much you need to come away from the noisiness and pressures of life. He even needed a retreat every once in a while. So, He went away from the maddening crowds to spend time in His Father's house, in the garden, or at the lake. Jesus knows that living on this planet can leave you spiritually bankrupt, emotionally drained, and physically exhausted. He knows that heavy, back-breaking load you are bearing is getting more and more cumbersome with every step. This sort of load makes you feel like the weight of the world is on your shoulders.

Do you feel your body getting wearier with every step? Take heart, my friend. Jesus knows how it feels to carry the weight of the whole world on His shoulders. He experienced this all too well when He carried the cross up Calvary's hill to be crucified for the sins of the world. Jesus conquered death, hell, and the grave so that you could have salvation and enjoy a new, abundant life through Him.

Jesus is your supply. Your job may give you a paycheck, but Jesus is your source. You might have a good health plan, but Jesus gives you well-being. Stuff and things may make you happy for a moment or two, but only Jesus can give you real joy. You might even have a nice house, but only Jesus can make it the special place you want to come home to. In Matthew 11:28-30, Jesus invited those who struggled under the oppressive laws of religious tradition to lay their burdens down. He offered them, in exchange, a new life of freedom.

This is the invitation the world longs to hear. The Savior of the world says, "Come one, come all. Come and dine. Come and eat. Come and drink. Come and stay. Come and receive. Come rest in Me." If you are overworked, overstressed, or just plain "over it," come to Jesus. I think sometimes we put our love relationship with Him on a diet. It seems as if we are afraid to come to His table and eat, as though we are afraid to get a second, third, or fourth helping of His love.

> Jesus extends a personal invitation for you to step out of your position in the fast lane. He invites you to get off the endless treadmill of life.

Jesus invites us to come to Him. Whatever you need, you can come and receive it from Jesus right now. Come, get as much as you need from Jesus. Get filled up and be completely satisfied in His presence. He is your ultimate source of everything you need in this life. There's no need to fear; there's always plenty to go around at the Master's table. You don't have to worry about how much anything will cost. Jesus has already paid the price. And because your salvation and restoration cost Jesus everything, they cost you nothing. Every heavenly blessing that Jesus died and rose again for in order to provide for God's children comes to you free of charge.

Let me tell you a story about the way I've seen this truth in my life lately. My hubby, Charles, came home the other day with two little puppies. They are absolutely the cutest puppies on the planet! Buster Brown is a roly-poly, rambunctious, and playful little fellow with a rusty brown coat. Whenever he sees Charles or me coming up the walk he can't wait to get to us. Unable to contain himself, he runs right to us, happily wagging his tail all the way. He loves spending every moment he can with us. And we love spending time with Buster Brown.

Then there's Lil' Lady. She's black with a tan face and legs. Her paws and the tip of her tail look as if they were dipped in a bucket of white paint, complete with specks of white atop her little head. So tiny and painfully shy, Lil' Lady must have been the runt of the litter. Whenever she sees us coming, or anyone coming toward her for that matter, she runs and hides. She's skittish, apprehensive, and tentative. I call her name, gently inviting her to come to me, but she rejects my invitations. I've tried to get close enough to pick Lil' Lady up. But, I admit, I'm not as agile as I used to be, and before I can reach her she takes off running in the opposite direction. I've even tried feeding her from my hand to gain her trust. That doesn't work either. She won't respond to my invitations to love her and be her friend.

Not so with Buster Brown. That little fellow runs and jumps and dances at my feet. Just being together, walking through the yard or by the pond, is what we like best. He's learning the sound of my voice and my commands, no doubt about it. This little puppy enjoys my company, and I enjoy his. Being with him is a great lesson in what it feels like to have my own girl's best friend.

Lil' Lady, on the other hand, saddens my heart. Oh, if she could only understand that I want to be her friend too! If only she could know that I would never hurt her; she'd be so much happier—and I would be too. Lil' Lady rarely knows the joy of human touch or what it's like to eat from my hand. I want her to know that she doesn't have to run away and hide anymore. Until I win her heart, I'll do all I can to help her trust me. I long for the day when Lil' Lady finally realizes what she's been missing. I'm determined to win her over.

These two little puppies are teaching me a great deal about intimate friendship and unconditional love. They are helping me to see what it looks like to accept or reject the kind of invitation of a friend.

"Come, all you who are thirsty, come to the waters; and you who have no money, come, buy and eat! Come, buy wine and milk wihout money and without cost." (Isaiah 55:1 NIV)

Now, I have a better understanding of how it must break the Father's heart when we run from Him, neglecting sweet fellowship with Him. Dear one, don't let anything keep you from receiving everything you need in the presence of the Lord.

Your accuser, the devil, will do all he can to keep you from enjoying God's presence. If he can, he'll keep you distracted. He'll lie to you, trying to make you feel like being in God's presence is boring or useless. Your adversary will keep you busy tending to things that don't really matter, or he'll bind you up, making you feel guilty and full of shame. These are all tools that satan uses to keep you from enjoying the peace that can only be found in God's presence. You are welcome in God's presence. You are not in His way. You are not an aggravation or an irritation. You are not a burden or a problem. On the contrary! You are His delight. As His child, you bring Him immense joy and pleasure.

Whatever is missing or broken in your life, run into the Lord's presence to receive everything you need. You will find that He faithfully provides for you.

Read About His Love

Friend, I want to share with you Matthew 11:28-30 from *THE MESSAGE* to bring this truth home to our hearts.

Are you tired? Worn out? Burned out on religion? Come to me. Get away with me and you'll recover your life. I'll show you how to take a real rest. Walk with me and work with me—watch how I do it. Learn the unforced rhythms of grace. I won't lay anything heavy or ill-fitting on you. Keep company with me and you'll learn to live freely and lightly.

Which one of these are you today?

___ **tired**
___ **worn out**
___ **burned out on religion**
___ **you name it**

Read Isaiah 55:1 and write it below in your own words:

Where does this extravagant, unconditional love and invitation to rest meet you today?

Flip over to the New Testament to discover a common theme in the following passages: Mark 1:17-18, John 6:37, and Revelation 22:17. Then fill in the blank based on these promising Scripture passages.

When I am tired, weary, broken down, lost, kicked out, thirsty, desperate, Jesus invites me to _____.

Now, remember. If you think that "coming away" with Jesus means packing a bag and heading for the hills (although that is a wonderful proposition), it is not necessary, nor is it always expedient. Jesus invites you to come away right where you are: whether you are in the kitchen, in rush-hour traffic, or in the boardroom, bedroom, or bathroom. The Lord Jesus, by the presence of the sweet Holy Spirit, who is with you and alive in you, is calling to you—even in the middle of your workday. He's wooing you while you're at the ball game or running to catch a plane. Jesus is calling you to a new life . . . a lifestyle of complete peace and rest.

Pray About His Love

Let's talk to the Lord together, okay?

O gracious God and Father,
    Grant me ears to hear You, a heart to draw close to You, willingness to obey You, courage to trust You, faith to believe You, patience to wait for You, a song to praise You, and a life to glorify You. In the precious name of Jesus, I pray. Amen.

Be About His Love

At the invitation of the King of kings, the Lord Jesus, you are summoned into His presence. Not to be shamed or belittled, but to love and be loved. With this in mind, write a love letter to Jesus—either in the space below, in the journaling pages in the back of this book, or in your own journal. Exchange any heavy burdens you might bear for the light and easy love of Jesus. As you go about your day today, freed from worry, following Him, do something special and tangible that reminds you He is your ever-faithful provider and friend.

VIDEO VIEWER GUIDE

Promise #4: You have _____ you _____ in God.

We can put our full _____ and _____ in God.

You can enjoy a _____ _____ with God by spending time with Him—time in His _____.

God gives us _____ _____ _____ in the face of adversity.

When you are _____ to the Lord, your battles become His battles.

The formula for winning life's battles:

1. Possess courage to follow God's direction, obeying Him with your heart even when it doesn't make sense in your head.

2. Determine that no matter what may come, you will listen to the voice of God; and with confidence and obedience, be determined to do His will.

3. On a moment by moment basis, make a commitment to do what God has called you to do. Commit your life, your gifts, your works, your talents—and give it all to God, because He gave it all for you.

Week 5

YOU HAVE A GOD-GIVEN PURPOSE

You have been given only one opportunity to glorify God with your life. What are you doing with it? Some people drift like a boat without a sail, heading out to sea in deep, uncharted waters. But you must seize every moment, desiring to live each day to the fullest. It is God's will for you to enjoy a purposeful, satisfying life.

This week we will take a closer look at God's plan for you. I trust you will discover that, indeed, God has a wonderful plan that has touched every age and stage of your life. He has a specific plan for you to accomplish. As you seek and worship Him, you will be able to see His plan unfold. And as a result, you'll maximize your efforts. You'll discover what living the abundant life truly is all about. Oh, yes, as you walk out God's plan, you will experience His embrace, one that is just for you that goes all the way down to your bones.

This week, meditate on this promise: *Because God loves me and has a great plan for my life, I am a success.*

Scripture Memorization

Throughout the week, continue focusing on our memory verse, John 17:23 (NCV):

"I will be in them and you will be in me so that they will be completely one. Then the world will know that you sent me and that you loved them just as much as you loved me."

Continue using the index cards in visible places and reading the verse when you get up, throughout the day, and as you go to bed. Remember that another great way to memorize Scripture is to write or type it.

109

Day 1: Knowing God's Plan

Commit your actions to the Lord, and your plans will succeed.
Proverbs 16:3 NLT

Think About His Love

God created you because He wanted to have a close, meaningful relationship with you.

God has big plans for you. As believers, we want to know how to find God's plan for our lives. Maybe you have been wondering, *Who will I marry?* Or *Should I take the job?* Perhaps you're in a season of pondering, *Should I go away to college or attend the community college across town?* Maybe you are deciding whether to buy or rent a home. Oh, yes, there are many questions in life. The good news is God wants you to know His will and purpose for your life more than you do. He doesn't play hide-and-seek with you when it comes to discovering your unique purpose.

You make plans to do this or that, or to go here or there. But the only plan that really matters is the *one made for you* by the God who loves you. His plan goes back—way back to before you were born.

Because God loves you and wants you to enjoy every aspect of your life, He designed an intentional plan for you. He has carried you in His heart from the beginning of time. Long before you took your first breath, God knew your name. He knew everything that would happen in your life, even before the day you were born.

God's plan for you is always the best plan. Remember: *Father knows best*. When you want to know anything about your life, *just ask Him*. God knows everything there is to know about you. There is no need for you to check your horoscope. If you have been tempted to call a psychic, I hope you hung up the phone. That little piece of paper inside a fortune cookie is just that—a piece of paper inside a hollow shell. The God who created you has written your life story. *He has a predetermined plan for you—to be in relationship with Him.*

God created you because He wanted to have a close, meaningful relationship with you. Your primary purpose is to give God first place in your life and make Him your main priority. So, if you have been focusing only on what will make you happy in this life, you have the wrong focus. Your priorities are backwards, and you will stumble and fall before you can get solidly up on your feet. Instead, ask yourself, *How can I demonstrate my love for God with my life?*

Discovering God's plan for you begins with returning His embrace: finding Him and putting Him first. This goes against the grain of natural or earthly thinking and behavior. In fact, it is one of the great paradoxes of the Bible. Let's read what Jesus said in Matthew 10:39: "If your first concern is to look after yourself, you'll never find yourself. But if you forget about yourself and look to me, you'll find both yourself and me" (*THE MESSAGE*).

Take a car's navigation system, for example. Before the system can determine the route to an intended destination, it must first orient itself by finding true north. Then after the system's inner compass hones in on true north, it points the driver in the right direction as he or she journeys along. So, you must orient yourself to God's absolute truth that life is not merely about what makes you happy. You discover true happiness while doing what brings pleasure to God. Your inner spiritual compass points you straight to a loving, obedient relationship with your heavenly Father through His Son, Jesus Christ. This is true north for you and me. This is the spiritual compass point where discovering our true life's purpose begins.

Let me tell you a story about some plans that came to be for me. After living in Metropolitan Atlanta for twenty-two years, Charles and I decided after the children were grown and on their own that we'd find a nice, quiet piece of land in the country and then settle down and enjoy the peaceful life. We found a few acres in rural Georgia where Charles could raise vegetables and I could plant flowers. We wanted a piece of property where we could fish every once in a while. That way, when we weren't on the road, we could enjoy our rest at home.

We decided on what kind of house we'd build on our farmland. But long before one shovel of dirt was turned over or any cement was poured, we had to have a plan for our home. We scoured books and magazines looking for just the right home design to suit our needs and desires. We visited numerous beautiful homes, took lots of pictures, and made plenty of notes.

On the day we went to meet with the home designer, we took all of our notes, pictures, and ideas. We liked the kitchen layout from one picture and the family room design from another. We wanted a great room with lots of space for family, friends, and of course, grandchildren. I wanted a room for my piano where I could write songs, and Charles desired a space where he could store seeds and farm tools.

After several visits we were excited when our designer presented us with the plans—the blueprint for our new country home. And the plans she presented to us weren't copies of any other home she had designed. They were unique to us: custom drawn with our needs and preferences in mind.

Once construction started I was amazed that our builder could determine how much cement, lumber, nails, and other building materials would be needed, just by studying those house plans. Soon, paint went up on the walls, and carpet went down on the floors. Then our hopes and dreams moved in with the furniture. By following the plan, our house grew from being a drawing on a piece of paper to a lovely home for our family to enjoy for years to come.

You are custom-designed: fearlessly and wonderfully created on purpose to fulfill a divine, God-given purpose.

The same is true for you. You were born as a result of God's predetermined plan for your life. Your strengths and weaknesses, likes and dislikes, hopes and dreams were all placed in you by God's design.

If I wanted to know the reasoning behind a particular invention, I'd talk with the inventor, wouldn't you? I would learn the story behind the invention and find out why the inventor was compelled to make such an object. Great inventors and designers each have a vision, a purpose, and a plan for their creations. Ground-breaking inventions such as the automobile, airplane, light bulb, microwave oven, telephone, bulldozer, and Frisbee, were invented with specific purposes in mind. In the same way, your heavenly Father conceptualized you in His mind, formed you with His own hands, and placed you here on earth to fulfill a specific purpose. Doing anything short of God's purpose would be a misuse (or even abuse) of His intention for your life.

You are a unique treasure: a masterpiece of God's design. That old saying is true: *when God made you, He broke the mold.* Truly, you are a distinctive expression of God's creativity in the earth. When God designed you, He placed within you certain gifts and abilities that are unique to who you are. He gave you desires and dreams that will help you to pursue His will and purpose throughout your life. When God empowers and equips you to accomplish His plan, you don't ever have to go it alone. Because where God guides He surely provides.

We often question why people are the way they are: why they possess natural abilities or a particular bent toward a certain quality. Maybe you love cooking or chemistry, languages or art. I have a friend, Jill, who designs wonderful clothes. When I need a special outfit for a certain occasion, I pay her a visit. Whenever I arrive at Jill's warehouse, I pick from an array of beautiful fabrics she has to choose from. Within an hour or two, I walk out with an outfit, customized just for me. Every time I wear one of her outfits, I get compliments from people wanting to know where these stunning, one-of-a-kind creations originated. I'm able to give credit to whom credit is due. There's no doubt, my friend Jill was born to sew.

Now, please don't ask me to sew anything. But sit me down in front of a piano, place a microphone on the stand, and you'll watch me come alive! I'll sing and play that piano until my heart is content because that is what I was born to do.

This same creative principle applies to you. God has given you gifts and abilities that come alive when you are in your element. As you flow in your God-given gifts and abilities, your genius is put on display. When you do what you were born to do, you shine like a star.

More than this, when you are flowing in your purpose it doesn't feel like work at all. Dear friend, that unique ability you possess didn't just happen. You are custom-designed: fearlessly and wonderfully created on purpose to fulfill a divine, God-given purpose.

Read About His Love

God made each of us for a unique purpose.

Read Psalm 32:8-9. Draw a basic timeline of your life in the space below, marking each decade as well as significant events and experiences of your life. Circle any times or situations when you felt God instructing, teaching, and leading you in the way you should go.

"Before I formed you in the womb I knew you, before you were born I set you apart." (Jeremiah 1:5 NIV)

Now, look at Jeremiah's call again (we first considered his call in Week 1, Day 4). In Jeremiah 1, God calls a young boy to become a prophet. Read Jeremiah 1. Then, complete verse 5 below as if it were a word from God to you.

Dear _____,

Before I formed you in the womb I _____ you, before you were born I _____ _____ _____. (Jeremiah 1:5 NIV)

Another promise is found in Jeremiah 29:11. Write your name in the blanks and read the promise aloud to yourself. Claim this promise and let it claim you today.

"For I know the plans I have for _____ ," declares the LORD, "plans to prosper _____ and not to harm _____ , plans to give _____ hope and a future." (Jeremiah 29:11 NIV)

In Matthew 10:39, Jesus tells us that the goal of life isn't to find ourselves but to find Him. And, when we find Him, that's right where we find ourselves. Where have you been looking to "find yourself"?

"The one who calls you is faithful, and he will do it." (1 Thessalonians 5:24 NIV)

What would change in your life if you looked first to Jesus for your purpose and identity?

Read Proverbs 16:13. This verse tells us that we will find success when we commit our plans to the Lord. What are your plans for your life?

How will you commit those plans to the Lord?

Write 1 Thessalonians 5:24 on an index card and work on committing it to memory as you continue memorizing John 17:23. Remember that God does not call you to a place where He is not. And He will not guide you without providing for you every step of the way.

Pray About His Love

I wrote this prayer along the same theme as Psalm 139. Will you pray this with me?

Lord, You search me and You know me
When I sleep and when I rise
You know everything about me
Right down to the color of my hair and eyes

Long before I came into being
Before the moment of my birth
You fashioned me with loving kindness
Gave me a purpose, value, and worth

Such knowledge is too much for me
That You would know my length of days
I will praise You, Lord, for the promise
That I'm fearfully and wonderfully made

This is my prayer, dear Lord,
In the name of Jesus I pray. Amen.

Be About His Love

Here is a simple assignment for today: go on a short walk with a friend. If you live in different cities, then connect by cell phone. As you walk, pray with one another. Talk about how much God loves you, what He's doing in your life, and how you are walking out His plan. Record any answers to prayer, insightful ideas, or confirmations of His will in the space below, or if you need more space, in the journaling pages at the back of this book.

DAY 2: CREATED TO WORSHIP

Let every thing that hath breath praise the Lord.
Psalm 150:6 KJV

Think About His Love

If you ever wonder what you were created for, look no further. I have the answer for you: you were created to praise and extol your Creator, Father God. As a matter of fact, all of creation has been designed with an inherent need to worship Him. You were put here on earth to bring glory to God, both in and through your life. Everything you do that brings glory to God is an act of worship. Our spiritual act of worship is to please God with all that is in us.

Oftentimes, we define worship as being confined to a place or a day of the week. Some people might even define worship as a style of music or the tempo of a song. But God defines worship as a lifestyle of commitment and obedience. This means in everything you do—in your conversations, relationships, work, and even leisure—you should be focused first and foremost on pleasing God as an obedient daughter in His kingdom on earth. Whatever you do as a result of your conscious love walk with God, desiring to please the Lord, He receives as an act of worship.

Johann Sebastian Bach is a great example of what it looks like to glorify God through one's work. He was one of the greatest composers in the history of Western music. A man of great faith, Bach believed that music was to be "a refreshment to the soul." He was persuaded that music was to be used as a tool to proclaim the gospel. Bach believed music should bring glory to God, and to demonstrate this belief, he signed most

of his scores with the statement "Soli Deo gloria"—"To God alone be the glory."[3] What a beautiful display of worship.

Too often *we worship our work, we work at our play, and we play at our worship.* We have gotten things completely out of order from God's intended purpose. If we don't consciously become more mindful of this, we will worship created things instead of the Creator who made them. Here's the bottom line. The Bible may not tell you specifically who to marry, what job to take, or whether to rent or buy your home. But the word of God will always tell you how to tune your heart and align your life, so you can recognize God's ultimate best when you see it.

In Week 3, I shared with you my "Four M's of Prayer." Today, I want to share with you my "Four W's of Walking in His Purpose." Try to keep them closely in mind, today and every day.

1. To know God's will, devote your time to reading His WORD. God's will is found in His WORD. The Bible is your spiritual compass. It is where you find God's instructions to live a life that is pleasing to Him.

2. To know God's will, develop an intimate WALK. Knowing God's plan for your life means first getting to know Him: the Author of the plan. Putting first things first, you must know God personally through His Son, Jesus Christ, to begin walking in His plan. Look at it this way. *No God, no purpose. Know God, know purpose.*

3. To know God's will, delight in His WAYS. If you want to know the ways of God, look at the life of Jesus. Do you want to please God? Live like Jesus. Do you want to develop lifelong relationships and influence people? Lead like Jesus. Do you want to be a blessing to people and serve well? Love like Jesus.

4. To know God's will, dedicate your life through WORSHIP. Honor God by living a life of obedience. It doesn't matter how many times a week you go to church or how many Christian songs you know. God is concerned about one thing—your love for and obedience to Him. Your daily life can be a wonderful act of worship if you live it to the glory of God.

Earlier I told you about my friend Jill and her ability to design and sew beautiful garments. God has given her a wonderful gift to create a designer's original in a matter of minutes. I can appreciate her skill and her meticulous attention to every detail. And you know what? I am in no way jealous of Jill's ability to sew. Not even for a second. It's so easy to applaud her and cheer her on. Yes, I can even invest my hard-earned money to support her business endeavor.

Isn't that the way it should be? When you are confident in your own area of giftedness, you will not be envious of others. Instead, you will find it easy to applaud them for their efforts. I'm sorry to say this, but sometimes we as women secretly wish to sabotage our sisters when we see them doing well. This is not God's will for us, dear friend. We must be in the business of building one another up instead of tearing one another down. We can do much more together than we can do apart. Will you agree with me to do all you can to encourage your sister's efforts? Will you support her business endeavors with your prayers and with your finances? Don't talk her down. Talk her up! Don't discourage her. Encourage her! Don't just tolerate her—celebrate her! Can I hear an *amen* on that?

Knowing that God has a plan for me always leaves my heart at peace. Regardless of what happens during my day, I can rest assured that my life is securely in God's hands. Dear one, God doesn't love you because of what you give Him; neither does He want you to love Him because of what He can do for you. The Father desires true worship—loving devotion that is offered to Him with all one's heart, mind, soul, and strength. This is where we find true joy.

Read About His Love

Today, I want us to spend some time looking together in the book of Exodus. In chapter 32, the children of Israel confused their worship of the Creator with worshiping created things.

Read Exodus 32:1-4. What did the Israelites ask of Aaron?

What did Aaron do?

This is a prime example of misguided worship. The Israelites were too impatient to wait for God's absolute best for their lives. And His best for them was to have His presence in their midst. God's intention was for them to discover His plan and purpose by loving and walking in obedience to Him. Instead, they settled for a counterfeit way of worship. They came together and persuaded Aaron, their leader in charge, to abandon the ways of God. Sadly, Aaron and a large group of God's people turned away from God's plan and decided to do their own thing.

When people make a decision to do their own thing, sin isn't too far behind. Instead of obeying God's command to worship Him, the one and only true God, the Israelites were content to worship an idol that Aaron had made with materials from their own hands. Sadly, about three thousand men, their wives, and children were led into idol worship that day. They carelessly created and gave honor to a false deity: honor that was due to God alone.

Sound familiar? This is what our culture is doing today. Instead of living a life of obedience by loving and worshiping the one, true God, many people are content to worship other "gods"—whether they be houses, money, property, cars, entertainment . . . even

> The Father desires true worship—loving devotion that is offered to Him with all one's heart, mind, soul, and strength. This is where we find true joy.

other people. God is still saying the same thing about idols today that He said to His people back then.

Read Exodus 20:4-5a and write the verse below in your own words.

Worshiping false gods can be blatantly obvious and deceptively subtle. What are some of the ways we worship false gods in our culture?

Have you ever fallen prey to the lie that a created thing or experience is worthy of your worship—worthy to rule your time, energy, thoughts, longings, and choices?

God desires and delights in our love and obedience as we live our lives before Him in worship. He would rather us love and serve Him wholeheartedly every day than serve our own desires six days a week and then, out of obligation, perform our "religious duty" to Him one day a week. God desires for our acts of worship—each moment of our lives—to be given wholly to Him from loving, grateful hearts.

God didn't want the Israelites to bring sacrifices and offerings to Him unless their hearts were in it. He also doesn't want us to oblige Him by going through the motions. God wants us to love Him and, out of love, to obey Him. He doesn't want us to reduce our relationship with Him to mere religious form and ritual.

Read 1 Samuel 15:22 and write what you hear in the passage about true worship.

Sisters, I want to share with you a promise from God for those who live out their purpose to worship God with all of their heart, mind, soul, and strength.

Blessed are those who fear the LORD,
  who find great delight in his commands.
Their children will be mighty in the land;
  the generation of the upright will be blessed.
Wealth and riches are in their houses,
  and their righteousness endures forever.
                    Psalm 112:1-3 NIV

Pray About His Love

Let's pray together.

Dear sovereign God,

Thank You for giving me peace in my soul concerning Your will for my life. The more closely I walk with You, the more I desire to do Your will. And the more I saturate my mind with Your Word, the more strength I find to accomplish Your purpose. Please, Lord, keep my mind free of clutter and my heart free of compromise. I want to live my life Your way. Guide me by Your truth today and every day of my life. In Jesus' name I pray. Amen.

Be About His Love

Pause for a few moments and think about God's great plan for your life. Consider the giftings and abilities He has given you . . . just because He loves you. Now consider: are you walking in God's purpose, unto Him, as an act of true worship? As the spirit of God moves in your heart, write a few notes in response to the questions below. Then take some time—now or later—to flesh out your thoughts in the journaling pages of this book or in your own journal.

What are you naturally good at?

What do you love to do?

What do people tell you that you have a gift for?

How does your life express these gifts right now?

How are you living a life of worship?

DAY 3: GOD IS WITH YOU

Where can I go from your Spirit? Where can I flee from your presence?
Psalm 139:7 NIV

Think About His Love

Success is not determined by *who you are.* Real success is determined by *who you are with.*

People all over the world have a drive to succeed. It doesn't seem to matter whether they live in a tiny farm community or in a huge metropolis. People want to lead a successful life. Oftentimes when we think of success and prosperity, we think of owning things like houses, automobiles, money, or other possessions. Of course, in and of themselves, there's nothing wrong with any of them; however, it's been proven time and again that things don't make people truly happy. Unfortunately, the headlines are filled with the sad stories of those who have chased after fame and fortune, only to find their pursuits empty and meaningless. Even some of the world's most widely recognized people have secured an infamous place in history, having lost their lives in the search of vain pursuits.

I'm persuaded that, deep down, people want more out of life—especially believers in the Lord, Jesus Christ. I'm sure you want your life to make a difference: you want it to be filled with real meaning and purpose. Ultimately, as a born-again, blood-bought believer with the breath of God stirring deeply in yourself, you want to carry out His plan for your life. You want to be truly successful.

God also wants you to be successful in every area of your life. But God's definition of success is different from the world's definition of success. According to God's Word, success isn't wrapped up in possessions, fame, or recognition. When you get right down to it, my friend, success is not determined by *who you are*. Real success is determined by *who you are with*.

One of my favorite Bible stories is found in 1 Samuel 16:14-18. It details what took place when a young man named David was called upon to serve King Saul. Every time I read it, my heart is blessed by seeing God's mighty hand on David's life, because I see how a great big God opened doors for a young shepherd who would become king of Israel. God's favor moved so mightily in David's life. The many psalms he wrote have found their way into countless songs and sermons. Even I have composed a number of songs that were inspired by the psalms of David.

David was a great psalmist whose music soothed the soul of a tormented king. He was an able hunter who killed wild beasts with his bare hands. As a brave warrior, he slew a giant with a slingshot and a single stone. David was the envy of men and the desire of women. But David's greatest asset didn't have anything to do with his talent. His finest qualities were not found in his acts of bravery or his good looks. Nor was David's most positive feature his popularity or what others said about him. The key to David's success was that God was with him.

You might be familiar with David's story. But let me give you a few details concerning his background. God had sent the prophet Samuel on a mission to Bethlehem to find and anoint Israel's next king. He had also told Samuel to offer a sacrifice there, inviting Jesse and his sons to attend. Unbeknownst to Jesse, the next king would come from among his sons. It was during this meeting that Samuel asked Jesse's sons to pass before him. Each son came and stood before the prophet. And each one was denied. I love what happened next. For whatever reason, David did not initially attend the sacrifice. Maybe it was because he was the runt of his brothers, too young to hang with the big boys. Maybe it was because he was a shepherd who smelled of sheep.

David's father didn't even recognize the significance of this moment. It's quite possible that Jesse was so caught up in the brawny outward appearance of his older sons—or maybe he was carried away in the moment by the invitation to be important people—that he didn't even seem to be concerned that his youngest son wasn't there. David's brothers probably thought he'd be in the way. But God doesn't think the way we think. God didn't just see David for who he was. He saw David for who he was destined to become. David's family saw him as the youngest child. God saw a great king, and a great king he was indeed. David became the greatest king Israel had ever known. Thousands of years later, he remains an icon—a symbol of success and accomplishment—to Israel and to the world.

There is a powerful lesson to be learned through David's great and miraculous story. Can you picture this young shepherd in the hills minding his father's sheep? Can you envision him singing at the top of his lungs, strumming a groove on his harp for an audience of dumb sheep? God surely saw him.

God considered David a huge success long before he ever became king. Even while David was performing the menial jobs of a shepherd, God took pleasure in him. He delighted in David's heart, causing him to be strengthened and his life to flourish. Even when David's family considered him a "nobody," God saw him as somebody. God saw greatness in him.

Because of what Jesus did for you on the cross, that same favor is already yours. As a rightful heir to the promises God made to Abraham, you have a right to each and every one of those promises as well. Now, remember, you can't earn God's wonderful favor in your life. You could never do anything to deserve it. It's God's free gift of love and grace to you, and the Giver finds great joy in presenting it to you. Your response should be to simply say thank you, open it up, and start enjoying it.

This, my friend, is amazing. Do you see how big God is? Never put a limit on His power and presence in your life. God is for you, not against you. He wants to help you, not harm you. There is nothing He can't do. There isn't a single adverse situation in your life that God can't use to bring about greatness in you.

As you assess your life today, don't define whether or not you are successful according to the world's standards. Don't determine you are or are not successful because of the things you either have or don't have. Don't compare yourself to others, gauging yourself against how they look or what they have accomplished. And one more thing, while we're here: Don't let your failures or setbacks define you. Only allow them to be a launching pad toward the great future that is out in front of you. Always remember that your best and brightest days are still ahead of you.

Determine you are a success for one reason only—because the Lord Jesus is with you.

When you allow God's great love to influence who you are, there are no limits to what you can accomplish. Knowing God changes your life and destiny. It doesn't matter what your occupation may be. As you yield your gifts and talents to God, He breathes on them. He blesses and multiplies them so that people are blessed and He gets the glory.

Read About His Love

David had a heart for God and knew that God was with him. Let's look at his story in 1 Samuel and let it speak to us today.

Read 1 Samuel 16:11-12. Why do you think Samuel wasn't interested in the other brothers?

Read 1 Samuel 16:14-18. Look closely at verse 18 and fill in the blanks below:

"One of the servants answered, I have seen a son of Jesse of Bethlehem who knows how to play the lyre. He is a brave man and a warrior. He speaks well and is a fine-looking man. And the LORD _____ _____ _____ ." **(NIV)**

Yesterday you prayed a prayer based on Psalm 139. Today I want us to look more closely at this psalm and fully realize God's constant presence with us. Read the psalm now and answer the following questions.

List the places and situations named in the psalm where God knows us and is present with us.

> As you yield your gifts and talents to God, He breathes on them . . . and multiplies them so that people are blessed and He gets the glory.

In what ways was David a success simply because he knew that God was with him?

Pray About His Love

Let's pray together.

Awesome God,

You are so amazing! You are concerned about every detail of my life. Nothing escapes You. Forgive me for ever doubting Your love and concern for me. There have been times I didn't understand the ways You were at work in my life, but, I know Your ways are perfect. Help me to trust You in every area of my life. From this day on, help me to depend fully on You to meet all my needs. More than this, Lord, stir up the gifts and talents You have given me. I thank You for each one—even those I am not yet aware of—and I present them to You anew today. Help me, as well, to be a source of encouragement to others as they exercise their gifts for You. From this day forward, help me to be defined not by my past mistakes, but by Your standard of success, and forgive me for ever looking to others for validation. I long for Your approval only, Lord. I understand that real success is found in You and You alone. Receive my heartfelt devotion today and always. In Your great name I pray. Amen.

Be About His Love

As you go about your day, observe how people around you long for success. Pay a little more attention to our culture's lust for material possessions. Think about it. Do things like television, music, and the Internet feed these desires in you? A relentless drive to acquire more things is evidence of an empty life. Remember: real success is the reality of God's presence in your life—because when you know God's plan and that He is with you, all things are possible.

Now, let's take it a step further. Turn off the television, take a break from the computer, and put on some inspirational music. Sit down in a quiet place to pray for friends and loved ones. Include someone special in your plans today. Instead of sending that usual, quick text message or e-mail, send a handwritten note or card to remind your friend of God's love and His incredible plan for his or her life. *Be about His love* today by sharing this wonderful blessing!

DAY 4: IN CHRIST, ANYTHING IS POSSIBLE

I can do all things through Christ who strengthens me.
Philippians 4:13 NKJV

Think About His Love

Friends, I want to urge you not to despise small beginnings.

If you had asked me when I was a young girl what I wanted to be when I grew up, I would have told you that I wanted to be a singer and a teacher. I even had a short-lived aspiration to be a spy. But the vocation of a professional composer was never on my list of things to become.

I have always been a lover of words and even wrote songs as a hobby when I was in college. However, it wasn't until after I attended a workshop in the early 1980s that the songwriting gift God had planted in me really began to flow out of me. I now know that the Lord divinely placed me at that conference. He ignited my songwriting gift at just the right place and time.

After that experience, I began to work at writing on my own and collaborating with other writers. Pretty soon, I was recording my compositions, and other recording artists were too. I'm living proof that we all possess gifts and talents that are lying dormant inside us.

I firmly believe there is greatness in you, just waiting to be brought to the surface. You possess ideas, solutions, creations, designs, books, masterpieces, recipes and inventions that God has divinely placed inside you. By God's great love and His amazing grace, He will place you right where He wants you to be, when He wants you to be there. Do you believe this?

Don't shy away from new opportunities. Seize them. Don't run from the challenge—run toward it. My father, the late Reverend George W. Wade, was a great preacher for forty years. He claimed some great words attributed to D. L. Moody as his life's motto, modifying them slightly: "If God be your partner, make your plans larger." God is for you, so think big. Though it may seem at times like you are small and insignificant, you can do great things for the Lord and the kingdom of God. Don't think for one moment that God can't use you. That small-minded, defeatist attitude is just what your adversary wants. You can accomplish any task that God calls you to complete.

I love Philippians 4:13. I call it the "Ten Finger Prayer." When I'm feeling overwhelmed or inadequate, I raise both hands, counting off each word as I recite it.

Then I surrender my challenge to the Lord. Try this exercise as you read it. Now, lay the book down and rest something weighty across the top margins, so you can read this verse hands-free. Are your hands up?

I can do all things through Christ who strengthens me. (NKJV)

Can't you just feel God's truth sinking in as your fingers move in perfect rhythm with your words? It makes me want to recite this verse again and again.

Regardless of your faults and foibles, God can and will use you to accomplish His purposes. Over and over again, He used people with challenges and weaknesses to demonstrate His great strength. Take a look at a short list of some of God's most unlikely characters:

Moses stuttered.
David was a murderer.
Jacob was a trickster.
Jeremiah was young.
Peter was known to have a short temper.
Matthew was said to occasionally dip into the treasury.
Mary was a teenage mother.
Abraham was old.
Sarah was cynical.
Naaman was a leper.
Jehoshaphat was outnumbered.
Thomas was a doubter.
Mary and Martha were impatient.
And Lazarus was dead.

Never say that you're too old, too young, unqualified, uneducated, not the right size or color, financially challenged—or any other excuse you may come up with—to accomplish great things for God. When you think and speak negatively about yourself, you defeat God's purpose in your life. Start agreeing with God. You must allow God to demonstrate His strength through your weakness by placing your life in His capable hands. *Who you are with makes all the difference in the world.*

My friend Dr. Tony Evans is a great preacher and master illustrator. When he speaks, I listen. He also serves as the chaplain for the Dallas Mavericks basketball team. In *Tony Evans' Book of Illustrations,* Pastor Tony shares a story about when he invited his family to join him at a Mavericks home game. The team was playing at Dallas's Reunion Arena, and Pastor Tony was scheduled to deliver the pregame devotional message to the team. He invited all of his family to join him for the big game and all the pregame activities. Then he tells about how he instructed them to caravan to the arena so they could all enter the arena as a group. The story goes something like this:

Be sure to park in the VIP parking lot. And should the gatekeeper question while you're parking there, just tell them you're with me. Enter the building through the VIP entrance at the rear of the building where the team members enter. And if anyone should question why they should let you in, just tell them you're with me.

Go on into the building and make your way to the dining room. There you'll find a wonderful dinner prepared just for you. Enjoy the meal. Eat all you want. Meet the team, their spouses and families. And if anyone should question why you're in there, just tell them you're with me. After dinner, go on into the room where we will hold the chapel service for the team, coaches, staff, and their families. Enjoy the service. And if anyone should question why you're there, just tell them you're with me.

After the chapel service, make your way into the arena. There you'll find the VIP section that has been reserved courtside for our family. You'll have the best seats in the arena. All your refreshments are on the house. And if anyone should question why you're in this section, just tell them you're with me.

And you see, you've been given every blessing, every privilege because of who you're with. And when you get to Glory and you stand before Almighty God, and He asks you why He should let you into His heaven, just stand real close to the Lord, the Author and Finisher of your faith and say, "I'm with Jesus."[4]

Success is not in who you know but in who knows you. True success comes only from having a real, life-changing relationship with Jesus. He knows the real you: your hopes, passions, and dreams. He loves your company and spending time with you. Jesus has given you the wonderful gift of your life's plan, and He wants you to walk it out.

Remember, you can do all things because Christ is your strength. You don't have to wonder if you are good enough, smart enough, rich enough, or popular enough. You don't have to wonder if you have the tools, the will, the power, or the might to do what God has called you to do. In Christ, you have everything you need to accomplish his perfect plan and purpose for your life.

Read About His Love

Philippians 4 is such a great reminder of learning to live out your purpose in Christ. Paul writes to the church in Philippi to encourage them to think about Christ, live for Christ, and do everything for Christ.

Read all of Philippians 4. Write every phrase that encourages you as you trust in Christ's strength for the work set before you.

Pray About His Love

Sisters, let's pray together that we would learn to trust Christ with His plans for our lives. We don't need to make excuses for why we can't do it; we just need to trust Him and live out those plans.

Dear heavenly Father,
You have loved us with such a perfect love. You know where we are and how we feel. You see through our excuses and our doubts. You love us still when we make our own plans, fail, and come running back to You. Show us Your perfect will in our lives. Fill us with Your strength to accomplish all that You ask of us. Help us walk boldly into Your purpose for our lives. We will give You all the praise and glory. In Jesus' sweet and precious name, we pray. Amen.

Be About His Love

With God, anything is possible. As you commune with God today, thanking Him for the great plans He has for you, remember to pray this promise for others, starting with your spouse, children, and/or extended family members, your pastor, church leadership, and so on. Then pray silently for those you pass along the way, such as the mail carrier, the grocery store clerk, and the daycare worker. The opportunities to share from God's banquet table are endless, so be generous. Share this blessing by praying it over as many people as you can today, so they'll come to know success God's way.

DAY 5: WHEN LIFE IS THE PITS

Why are you downcast, O my soul? Why so disturbed within me? Put your hope in God,
for I will yet praise him, my Savior and my God.
Psalm 42:11 NIV

Think About His Love

No matter what your present situation may seem to be, God promises your future is filled with hope: hope that is as bright as His deep love for you.

Never forget, beloved friend, you are God's favorite. He wants to prosper you more than you know because He loves you. A great big God is on your side. He wants to "open you the windows of heaven, and pour you out a blessing, that there shall not be room enough to receive it" (Malachi 3:10) as you follow His plan. In God, your future is brimming over with promise and pregnant with possibilities.

I'm sure there have been times, however, when life has been the pits: when things around you have appeared to be anything but hopeful. During these times it can be difficult to say there is hope. Hear me well, my dear friend; it's all too easy to slip into the miry quicksand of hopelessness and despair when circumstances seem to be just the opposite of God's best for you. But I want you to remember that as long as you have life, the very breath of God within you, there is always hope for you.

It may comfort you to know some things are common to us all. There are times when before we've hardly finished our morning cup of coffee, we've heard some sort of bad news. The long list of life's calamities can easily cause one's heart to sink. The daily newspaper and the twenty-four-hour-cable news channels have made it their business to tell us everything that's gone wrong in the world. Yet I say to you: Have hope in God!

Thinking back, I can remember many times when my mother (the pastor's wife) hung up the phone and said, "Lord, if it ain't one thing, it's another." She had just finished a long conversation with yet another hurting soul going through life's challenges. Life isn't easy. Denise, a friend of mine, has a variation on that theme. She says, "If it ain't one thing, it's two."

My dear mother and my friend are both right! If it's not your kids, it's the car. If it's not your house, it's your health. And if it's not your money, it's your honey. Sometimes it seems one's list of woes never ends. But let me assure you, there is good news for us, the good news of the gospel! Because Jesus finished His perfect work at the cross, no matter what things may look like, we have a great hope and a bright future.

You may have a long list of challenges, my dear friend, but God loves you. He has already made a way for you. And He wants you to be assured by faith that hope is not just around the corner. *Hope is right where you are.* Hope is *not* just a wish away. *Hope is available to you right now.*

In Christ, you don't have to give up or give in to life's challenges. You can get filled up with His presence and believe for a turn-around, try again, start over. . . . whatever the situation requires, you can do above and beyond that. Hope always rises above it all because God's grace is sufficient for your every need. His power is perfected in your weakness.

The devil knows this too. So, he works diligently to steal your hope. He tries to wear you down with constant attacks against your faith. He sends annoying distractions everywhere you turn. He shouts in your face about all the bad things that are happening both to you and around you. But you don't have to give in. Don't let the enemy steal your faith and hope in God. Run, don't walk to the Master. Receive grace and help in your time of need.

Dear friend, as long as you focus your energies on your own needs and circumstances, *your problems* will always seem bigger than *your God*. It's time we quit shouting our problems while whispering our praises. Can I hear an *amen*?

Each time your hope comes under attack, hope in the Lord. Rise above the weakness of your flesh, and submit to the counsel of God's Word. Then resist the devil, and what will happen? That lying, scheming, conniving adversary will have to flee (James 4:7). No matter what you may be facing, God gives more grace. The spirit is willing and the flesh is weak; so when your flesh rises up, humble yourself before God. He'll take it from there, and the devil will get out of your way.

As we discussed earlier in our study, a lot of people think of hope as being wishful thinking, a waiting game, presumption, betting, wagering, or wishing upon a star. They say things like, "I hope things will turn out okay," or "I hope we get some rain soon." But never forget the biblical definition of hope! It is much more than wishing, wondering, or wagering. Hope in God is a confident expectation of good based on our Father's perfect character and the integrity of His promises. Hope in God is a firm assurance concerning a situation that is otherwise unclear or unknown. Hope is complete confidence in God, believing Him for a favorable outcome.

When you hope in God you can see yourself blessed. Because you hope in the Lord, you can envision yourself healthy. Because of godly hope, you can see every one of your needs being provided for according to His riches in glory by Christ Jesus.

My friend, God's promises are from everlasting to everlasting. Even when you don't see any evidence of God in a situation, you can have the confident assurance that He's behind the scenes working all things together for your good. When everything seems to be going all wrong, God will cause your circumstances to work out all right. I've always said, "God never does something for nothing. He always does something for something!" With God, even your pain has a purpose. What the enemy means to work against you, God causes to work for you as you stand in faith!

One Sunday morning while I was getting ready for church, I turned on the television just in time to catch the last few minutes of a sermon delivered by one of my favorite pastor friends and great Bible teacher Andy Stanley. I didn't hear the entire sermon, but I'll never forget the words I did hear. Andy's words filled my heart with hope and encouragement.

Let me encourage you as I paraphrase from memory. He said that it is imperative on life's journey to keep walking by faith. Just keep putting one foot in front of the other. Don't look to the left or to the right. Keep your eyes on the goal. Don't get discouraged by people who are wandering aimlessly on the road. Don't be distracted by meaningless signs and billboards that are on the roadside. If the road is rough, just keep plodding forward. If the way is steep, just keep moving methodically, putting one foot in front of the other. You may or may not have an emotional experience with God during your journey. You may or may not have clear-cut directions. Just remain obedient. Wait for instructions, and then keep walking by faith. One day, your faith and God's faithfulness

Even when you don't see any evidence of God in a situation, you can have the confident assurance that He's behind the scenes working all things together for your good.

will intersect, and you will finally see with your natural eyes what you only believed by faith beforehand.[5]

Later that week, I was working on some interviews with a friend at a local radio station in a downtown high-rise. We took a break for lunch and headed down to the café in the lobby area of the building. While we ate lunch, I shared with my friend how Andy Stanley's sermon had impacted me and had given me hope regarding my circumstances. When I finished sharing the details of the sermon with my friend, we noticed a woman seated in the corner of the café. She was the only other person in the café besides us. Suddenly, she began to weep aloud at the table where she was sitting. Then her cries turned to sobs. Then from her sobs began to flow audible words of praise and thanksgiving to God.

Wanting to know what was going on, my friend and I got up and went over to her table to see if we could be of help. She shared with us that she had lost her job that day. And she was going to be evicted from her apartment. She had no money to feed her children. Then she said that for some reason she decided to come in to that café to escape the heat of the oppressive summer sun.

She didn't know what she was going to do about her situation. She prayed a prayer of desperation to God. She told us that if she didn't hear from Him soon that she was planning to just go home and find a way to end her life. The sweet woman said while she was crying out to God in her pit of despair, she heard the words of hope coming from across the room. That's when she leaned in and eavesdropped on our conversation. Hope rose up inside her as she listened to our words of faith in God.

My friend and I were amazed! I wish you could have seen the three of us as we embraced. Then the three of us applauded God, shouted praises to Him, and cried tears of joy. Then my friend and I thanked God for sending the word of hope our sister desperately needed to hear. We affirmed to her that God was on her side and that He had divinely directed her into that café. We bought her some lunch and blessed her with the cash we had in our pockets. Then we gave her phone numbers and contacts to agencies and people we thought could help her employment and housing situations. Finally, we assured her that if God could arrange that meeting in the café, He definitely had an answer for every detail of her situation.

Yes, that sister needed money for rent and food and a good job to replace the one she had just lost. But more than anything, at that moment, that dear lady needed hope. Remember, good friend, that you are dearly loved by Father God today and always. Everything you need is available to you through Jesus. He is your source of hope. When you feel that life is the pits and you've been forgotten or overlooked, be assured that God has not forgotten you. Neither should you forget Him, my friend.

Read About His Love

Let's do a little faith exercise. Let's practice looking to God and remembering His hope-filled promises, so you can do it on your own when the need arises. Because when you rehearse God's hope-filled truths, your problems diminish compared to the awesome greatness of Almighty God!

Look up these passages and write the promise or promises found in each.

Psalm 27:14

James 4:7

Galatians 6:7-10

Romans 5:1-5

Psalm 103:1-5

Wait for the LORD; be strong and take heart and wait for the LORD. (Psalm 27:14 NIV)

Pray About His Love

As you pray today, I want you to put your book down and turn your hands so that your palms are facing upward toward heaven. Now, open them wide to convey that you are ready to receive from the Lord.

Dear sweet Father in heaven,
Thank You for always hearing our prayers and for being attentive to our outward cries of frustration or our silent requests from a heart of brokenness. You are aware of every single need that Your children have. My hands and my heart are open to You

right now. I release every care for Your simplicity, every burden for Your easy yoke, every broken dream for Your promise of a bright future, every hurt for Your healing, and every pit for Your pinnacle. In exchange I receive Your help for my plans, Your grace for my weaknesses, Your love for my lack of charity, Your forgiveness for my sins, and Your acceptance for every time I have been rejected. Fill my heart with a buoyant hope and top it all off with a relentless joy that overflows into every area of my life. I give myself to You and pray in Jesus' name. Amen.

Be About His Love

When you receive a blessing from God, don't keep it to yourself; instead, turn and give it to someone else. In the words you speak, with the people you meet, whether the news they bring is good or bad, practice hope today. Joyfully sow what you have received from God, and you will reap rich rewards.

VIDEO VIEWER GUIDE

Promise #5: You have a _____ - _____ _____ in life.

God's plan for you is to be in an intimate, life-giving _____ with

Him. Your priority and purpose in life is to give God _____

_____.

God's plan for you is to _____ _____ with your whole heart—
with all of your life.

God's plan for you is to use your gifts and talents to _____

_____ _____ for your life.

If God is your _____, make your plans _____.

In God, there is _____ _____.

Week 6

You Can Accomplish Great Things in God's Name

If you were given the choice to have a real diamond or a fake one, which would you choose? I don't know about you, but I would say, "Give me the real thing!" There's a popular saying going around that tells you to "fake it 'til you make it." I say with Jesus on your side, you are more than a conqueror, and there's no need to put up a front. Why fake it, only appearing to possess victory in Jesus, when you can have the bona fide, real deal?

This week I want us to celebrate God's great power that is available to you and to me. This power that equips you to make a difference, to do the right thing, or even to do the impossible, is *in Christ,* and He is *in you.*

We need the bona fide power of God in the world today. Because only His anointing equips us to complete the task to which He has called us. And only His mighty power can break every yoke of bondage. Only His love can penetrate a world gone crazy and bring light and life to hurting, wounded, and wayward souls.

The Father wants His children to continually flow in His power, sharing His love in this lost and dying world. So, this week we'll meditate on this precious and powerful promise: *Because God loves me, He has given me the ability to accomplish great things in His name.*

Scripture Memorization

Throughout the week, continue focusing on our memory verse, John 17:23 (NCV):

"I will be in them and you will be in me so that they will be completely one. Then the world will know that you sent me and that you loved them just as much as you loved me."

Continue using the index cards in visible places and reading the verse when you get up, throughout the day, and as you go to bed. Remember that another great way to memorize Scripture is to write or type it.

DAY 1: TAKE A BIG LEAP OF FAITH

"Lord, if it is You, command me to come to You on the water."
Matthew 14:28b NKJV

Think About His Love

God wants you to put your faith into practice.

The story of the disciples' faith adventure, which took place in a violent storm on the Sea of Galilee, is powerful. Sometime between 3:00 and 6:00 a.m., Jesus appeared to His followers, calmly walking on the high, menacing waves. Thinking they had seen a ghost, the disciples cried out in fear. Their boat was being dashed and battered by angry waves on every side when Jesus spoke to them, telling them not to fear.

Always the audacious one, Peter shouted, "Lord, if it is You, command me to come to You on the water" (Matthew 14:28b NKJV). That's when Jesus called out to Peter and said, "Come" (v. 29).

This small yet powerful word is such a beautiful invitation. It says so many things, like "Don't go. Don't leave. You are not a burden. I can help you. You are not a bother. You are a friend. You are welcome. Come on." Peter immediately responded to the Lord's invitation.

Of course, later in the story, Peter's trust wavers just enough to send him sinking into the waves, but Jesus was right there to pull him out. Peter is often looked down upon because fear gripped his heart and he began to sink. But in my opinion, Peter deserves a standing ovation. While the other disciples cowered in fear, clinging to one another inside the boat, Peter was the only disciple who dared take a huge step of faith and get out of it. Peter will go down in history for defying gravity; he actually walked on water!

Peter is a shining example for us all. We should all pray to receive more of the ridiculous courage Peter had—courage to move beyond predictable boundaries and take a big faith step into deeper, seemingly troubled waters. It's easy to stay safe inside the boat. But I can hear Peter cheering us on to step out and trust Jesus to do more, even if the circumstances seem to be way over our heads. If for some reason we fall or even fail as we walk toward Him, Jesus will gladly rescue us with His strong, dependable arms.

It's interesting. None of the other disciples had enough faith in Jesus to get out of the boat, so Peter left them behind. Peter did what he had to do completely on his own, alone.

If you are going to follow Jesus, at some point you will have to leave familiar surroundings and the comfort of the crowd. Your decision to take a risk may not always be popular. Others may try to discourage you and suggest that you take an easier way, but hear me: you will never grow in faith listening to the naysayers—and naysayers there always will be! As you step out in faith toward God there will be people in your life who say, "You're crazy to think you can walk on water. It's way too risky. The timing isn't right. Hurry! Get back in the boat!"

But don't be swayed by their discouraging words. Don't allow yourself to be so distracted by people that you miss the faith adventure of a lifetime. Don't be anxious to do what everybody else is doing, or you will miss the joy of journeying with Jesus to intimate places where few people choose to go. No, my friend; you must choose to be different.

Many times, it may not be easy to step out into unfamiliar territory. When you take that big leap of faith, you don't always know how or where you will land. Sometimes disappointment, discouragement, love, and loss will work their way into the tapestry of the story. And so it was with a young Irish hymn writer by the name of Joseph Scriven.

Joseph Scriven was born in Dublin, Ireland in 1819, into a family of material means. At age twenty-five he decided to leave his family and immigrate to Canada, where he met a beautiful young woman. They intended to be married; however, on the eve of the wedding, his bride-to-be accidentally drowned. Mr. Scriven, a generous and compassionate man, threw himself into his work, helping the poor and disenfranchised people of that day. Love would give him another chance. He met another young lady and they would be engaged to be married. Tragically, his fiancée suddenly fell ill of pneumonia and died, leaving him stricken with grief.

In 1855, Joseph Scriven received word from his homeland of Ireland that his mother had fallen deathly ill. To comfort his mother, he wrote a poem for her. The poem was titled "Pray Without Ceasing." That poem was later set to music and renamed by his dear friend, Charles Converse. The lyrics and music have become a favorite source of comfort for millions around the world and is known today by the title "What A Friend We Have In Jesus." A monument commemorating the life of Joseph Scriven was erected in Port Hope, Ontario. He will always be known as a friend to the poor and needy, and a friend in the Lord Jesus.

The second stanza of this timeless hymn is of significance in our exploration of taking a leap of faith. Scriven's words vividly describe how every believer must feel when the decision has been made to step out into the unknown.

Don't be anxious to do what everybody else is doing, or you will miss the joy of journeying with Jesus to intimate places where few people choose to go.

Have we trials and temptations?
Is there trouble anywhere?
We should never be discouraged,
Take it to the Lord in prayer.
Can we find a friend so faithful?
Who will all our sorrows share?
Jesus knows our every weakness,
Take it to the Lord in prayer.

Words: Joseph M. Scriven (1819–1886)
Music: Charles C. Converse (1834–1918)

Let these great words encourage you to keep looking out in front of you, just as Peter did when he got out of the boat. God is already there. Jesus has empowered you. The Holy Spirit is guiding you, and the angels are watching over you. Remember: many people see, but not everyone has vision. Keep your head, and don't let what is around you distract you.

As your confidence in Christ grows day by day, you'll become more confident in your vision and direction. Don't get it wrong here. Your confidence is not *in who you are,* but in *whose you are.* When you focus on *whose you are,* you will find yourself moving from where you are right now to where you are called to be.

Now, lean in a little closer and listen more intently. Do you sense Jesus calling you to take a leap of faith? If so, what are you waiting for?

Read About His Love

Peter shows us so much about the journey, from excited and childlike trust, to doubt and fear, and finally to receiving the grace needed to get back up again.

Read the entire story of the faith journey that led Peter out of that boat in Matthew 14:22-33.

What did Jesus say in verse 27?

How did Peter respond to the man on the water (verse 28)?

What did Jesus say to Peter that got him out of the boat (v. 29)?

What happened when Peter noticed the wind (v. 30)?

What did Peter cry out (v. 30b)?

How did Jesus respond to Peter's plea (v. 31)?

What was the response of the group once Peter and Jesus returned to the boat (vv. 32-33)?

Just like Peter, greatness lies deep within you. God has given you an assignment, and it's up to you to gain a clear understanding from Him of just what that assignment is. Once you have an understanding, pray for faith, vision, wisdom, strength, and obedience to get out of your boat and do it. Years ago, I learned an acronym for the word *faith*. Memorize it and recall it when you need it.

Forsaking
All
I
Trust
Him

Pray About His Love

God's love is sure, and He always has the answer. Let's talk to God about the challenges you are facing and the "deep water" that is out in front of you:

Dear faithful Father,
    Thank You so much for loving me. I am so grateful that Your love for me is bigger than the challenges I am facing now or may face tomorrow. I confess that sometimes

I am overwhelmed by my circumstances. But what a friend You are to me! When my circumstances are over my head, I know they are under Your feet! I thank You that I don't have to be anxious about a single thing, but I can bring all my requests to You. You will exchange my doubts for faith and replace my fears with courage. Thank You for the confidence I have in You, regardless of what I face today. In Your sweet name, I pray. Amen.

Be About His Love

It's easy to stay inside the boat. But Jesus loves you and wants you to trust Him with every storm in your life. Take a step of faith and trust Him with more, even if the circumstances seem to be over your head. Now consider: What does getting out of the boat look like in your situation? In the space below, briefly describe a vision for what it would mean for you to step out of the boat in this season of your life. When you have time, develop your thoughts in the journaling pages in this book or in your own journal.

DAY 2: STAGE A COMEBACK

Then some Jews came from Antioch and Iconium and won the crowd over. They stoned Paul and dragged him outside the city, thinking he was dead. But after the disciples had gathered around him, he got up and went back into the city.
The next day he and Barnabas left for Derbe.
Acts 14:19-20

Think About His Love

God's mighty power equips you to get back up as often as life's challenges knock you down.

It is always a very humbling experience to hear how a song that I've written has impacted someone's life in a real and profound way. It's the prayer of my heart that God would use the songs from my recordings to touch the hearts of people right where they are living. A young man, we'll call him Ian, worked as the church audio engineer and shared his story during our sound check before a concert that would take place at his church. Ian told me that he had been strung out on drugs since he was a young kid. But after years of using and abusing, he had gotten fed up with the reckless cycle of addiction. He had been on and off drugs, in and out of jail, and he was tired of walking through the revolving door that led to nowhere. So Ian decided to get off of drugs.

Ian had accepted Christ and was in drug abuse counseling for the third time in an effort to quit using. His older brother was providing transportation for him to get to and from his group meetings, since Ian had lost his license after being stopped for driving while intoxicated. One night Ian felt the strong desire to use drugs. He decided to throw in the towel, take his brother's car, and go find drugs. When he got into the car and turned the key to start the ignition, a song began to play on the CD that was already in the player. The words of the song captivated Ian's heart and spoke to his deepest need as only the Lord can. (If you attended the group session for Week 3, these words will be familiar to you because you heard them at the close of the session.)

Sometimes you rise and sometime you fall
Sometimes you wonder if you'll make it at all
But when you are weakest, that's when I am strong
So here's a promise you can rest on

I love you, I love you, I love you, I do
I love you through the darkest of night
And in the daytime too
Just as roses are red and the violets are blue
Never doubt for one moment that my love is true
But should you need to be reminded of how I feel about you
I'll tell you again, I love you, I do . . .

I love you from the crown of your head to the sole of your feet
And I did before I knit you together
I love you from high on a Hill where I laid down my life
*So you could be with me 'til forever**

Ian sat there in the car in the middle of the dark night and wept, knowing that God knew exactly where he was as well as the tremendous hardship of his personal struggle. That was a defining moment in Ian's journey and a U-turn on his road to recovery. It wasn't by any means easy, but Ian kicked his drug habit with the help of God and a big brother who loved him through it all. Today he runs a residential home for men with life challenges such as drug and alcohol abuse. From his own painful experience, he is allowing God to use him to bring others to victory. Ian is a true overcomer.

When you have been stretched to the breaking point, God always has a way of propelling you to even greater possibilities.

To know that this song helped Ian through a very real and personal struggle is an amazing testament to God's great ability to orchestrate all manner of details to get to the one He loves. I pray that "I Love You, I Do" speaks to you as well. I chose to include it as part of this study to remind you of God's never-ending promises to be with you always and to love you through it all, no matter what.

The truth is that life can pull the plug on you without so much as a moment's notice. But when the circumstances of life knock us down, God empowers us and helps us to get up and get going again.

Let me emphasize, dear friend, that though the enemy can't destroy you, he would like to leave you wounded and broken on the battlefield of life as an example to the world. Interestingly, I have heard that in military combat the land mine was primarily designed to cause injuries because it takes two able-bodied soldiers to transport one disabled trooper. So, three are incapacitated and removed from combat. But when a soldier is killed in battle, another soldier simply removes his dog tag and keeps on fighting.

Satan will try to take us down when he cannot take us out. But in Christ, our strength is renewed.

Trouble can arise unexpectedly when things are going well. Often, it seems that when we are riding the crest of success, happiness, and well-being, the earth shifts, and we find ourselves standing on the stage alone, vulnerable, while the whole world watches. We build that dream home and a year after we move in, the real estate bubble bursts, property values plummet, and the mortgage we owe is greater than the value of the home. We finally reach retirement age and are posed to enjoy the golden years when the doctor tells us that the test results from lab work say a tumor is malignant. After successfully completing training for a better-paying position at work, we are notified that the company is downsizing, and we will be facing an indefinite layoff. For some, it seems their marriage couldn't be better when they discover their spouse is having an affair. Life is filled with situations that can knock you down and leave you feeling mortally wounded.

But when you have been stretched to the breaking point, God always has a way of propelling you to even greater possibilities.

One time while I was doing some housekeeping, I spotted a rubber band lying on the floor. When I picked it up, the kid in me emerged, so I pulled back on the elastic band and shot it. Just then, the Holy Spirit prompted me to engage in an exercise I now call "rubber bandology," or the study of the rubber band. When I pulled back gently on the band and released it into the air, it didn't go very far. I picked it up again. Only this time, I pulled back a little harder, applying more pressure on the band. When I released it, it flew out in front of me a little farther. Once more, I picked it up. This time I pulled back as far as I could, stretching it to the limit, without breaking it. When I released the rubber band, it lofted high into the air and went sailing across the room.

The Lord reminded me that to the degree that life's situations pull on my patience, put pressure on my finances, push against my marriage, stress my health, and stretch my faith to the limit—to that same degree and more—I will be launched into the next season of greatness in my life. The process may be uncomfortable. It may even be painful. But God is faithful.

God loves us so much that He always causes our challenges to work for us, not against us. In Christ, what may appear to be a setback is not a setback at all. *It is a setup for a comeback!* Every challenge is a launching pad for success. It's another opportunity to experience God's power in your life!

Read About His Love

The Apostle Paul faced a situation where his very life was at stake. But the Lord came to the rescue for Paul, just as He has for me, for you, and for so many others on countless occasions. Let's take a closer look at one of Paul's amazing stories.

Read Acts 14 in its entirety and work through the following questions. Write down any insights, questions, or applications that the Holy Spirit reveals to you.

What was the work that Paul and Barnabas were called to do? (vv. 1-10)

What were the obstacles they faced along the way? (vv. 2, 11-19)

How did Paul and Barnabas respond to the opposition? (vv. 14-17, 20)

What did they do after this event? Check all that apply. (vv. 20-28)

___ **Called it quits.**

___ **Got up and got back at it.**

___ **Continued preaching the good news and winning disciples.**

___ **Shared their testimony with other churches.**

The account of Paul and Barnabas's first missionary journey tells of their experience in Lystra, where Paul was stoned, presumed dead, and dragged from the city to be left out as buzzard bait. But that wasn't the end of Paul's story! With God on our side—praise God!—we are never down for long.

Are you feeling knocked down and dragged out? Are you feeling like calling it quits? How does this story of Paul and Barnabas speak to you today?

Pray About His Love

Today is a great day to stage a comeback, don't you agree? If life has dealt you a low blow, bringing you down to your knees, always remember—you don't have to stay down. With the help of God, you can pull yourself up, brush yourself off, and press on. Let's make the prayerful words of another great hymn writer, Martin Luther, our own:

Dear heavenly Father,

I call to you from deepest need,
O Lord, hear my request.
I know I've sinned in word and deed,
But now I'm in distress.
Please overlook my errant ways,
And gaze at me with tender grace,
And help me fix this mess.
In You, dear Lord, I place my trust,
I've soured on self-reliance.
Your Spirit arms each one of us
To slay our taunting giants.
Your promises prove strong and true,
And I'd be nothing without You.
I pledge my full compliance.[6]

Amen.

Be About His Love

Has the bottom ever dropped out of your plans, leaving you holding the bag—only to have Jesus come and deliver you? Remember that today's test is tomorrow's testimony.

Think about the details of a recent event in your life and form it into a story to tell. Even if the end of the story is unresolved, leave room for a faith-filled outcome. Share this "test-imony" with your spouse, your children, or a friend today. It will encourage them to hear it and encourage you to share it with everyone you know.

DAY 3: AVOID SELF-PITY

When Jesus saw him stretched out by the pool and knew how long he had been there, he said, "Do you want to get well?"
John 5:6 CEB

God's loving forgiveness always allows us to forgive ourselves.

Think About His Love

Yesterday we talked about staging a comeback and we celebrated together that God launches us forward when we have been set back. Today I want to look at the process of the comeback and one of the dangers of falling into the pit: self-pity.

The first step in the process, after begin knocked down, is simply to get up. Don't wallow in the mire and throw a pity party. No one will come to join you anyway. People don't want to come to pity parties. Don't put on the cloak of guilt. That's one little black dress you don't even need to try on. Don't become paralyzed by fear. Realize what's happening, and look it square in the face. Self-pity, guilt, and fear are arrows that the enemy uses to wound your spirit and render you ineffective.

Remember that satan is the great accuser. In the story of the woman caught in adultery, her accusers brought her to Jesus, and Jesus dismissed them with a challenge for the one who was without sin to cast the first stone. Then He showed compassion, mercy, and grace to the woman. I like to imagine that she walked with confidence out of that situation—not with self-pity. If Jesus could forgive her, surely she could forgive herself and refuse self-pity.

God's loving forgiveness always allows us to forgive ourselves.

There are many times when our suffering is self-inflicted by sin in our lives. We develop a pattern of disobedience, and the consequences of our behavior cause anguish, leaving us with a tremendous burden of guilt. You can't make a big comeback dragging a load of either guilt or self-pity behind you.

Self-pity is a highly poisonous dart in satan's quiver. It robs us of our dignity and self-worth. In the Gospel of John, chapter five, we find the account of a man who had been sick for thirty-eight years and was lying by the pool of Bethesda. As the story goes, at a certain season an angel went down into the pool and stirred up the water; whoever stepped in first after the stirring of the water was healed of whatever disease he had (vv. 2-6). Often, Bible readers assume this man had been lame because Jesus told him to pick up his bed and walk. The text, however, does not say that had been his condition. It says that he was sick. Jesus knew the man had been in that condition a long time and asked him if he wanted to be made well. And, like a lot of us do, he had a little pity party. He told Jesus that people kept cutting in front of him and there was no one willing to help get him into the healing waters.

If we look closely at this story, we discover some interesting insights into this man's personality. Jesus asked him a direct question. The man responded with an excuse. His response was not the expected unequivocal yes! He gave Jesus an excuse that placed blame outside himself and declared his own helplessness and inability to compete. In effect, he said, "I am worse off than the others, and furthermore, I've been facing this challenge all by myself. I have no one to put me in the water."

Not only was this docile man waiting for the miraculous "stirring of the water," he was also awaiting an unexplained appearance of an unidentified benefactor. This able rescuer would overlook all the other needy individuals, select him out of the crowd, pick him up, rush him into the pool (ahead of everyone), and place him safely in the healing waters.

Once I was approached by a young man addicted to crack cocaine. He asked me for money and quickly followed his request with an explanation. He said, "I've got a drug habit, so don't preach to me about how I need to change. I enjoy getting high, and when I get tired of begin an addict, then I'll quit. But right now all I need is a little help. Could you spare two dollars?" There are many in our society today who are comfortable in their sickness. For them, healing could require getting a new job, becoming a responsible person, perhaps raising a family, and taking control of their own lives.

People become addicted to many substances and behaviors, including food, sex, and impulsive spending. Although they overtly claim to want deliverance, they are quietly satisfied with their condition. We see Jesus not inquiring but confronting the man at the pool. He saw a passive man who had brought a bed and found relative comfort in joining a community of incapacitated individuals. So He asked him, "Do you [really] want to be made well?"

Jesus is asking the same question today: "Do you want to be healed?" If you are standing passively by while healing and wholeness keep bubbling up in front of you, Jesus would challenge you to rise up out of self-pity. He would tell you that if you really want to bounce back after a setback, if you really want to rebound from a guilty past, if you really want to overcome fear—then you must choose to get up. Jesus would challenge you to assume a measure of responsibility and exercise self-control, so you can master the circumstances that once mastered you.

When life has knocked you down, you must let your desire for healing be the driving force that propels you far away from an attitude of helpless codependency.

Though your strength may be limited, you must use this measure of strength to lift yourself up from that position of self-pity, guilt, fear, complacency, and comfortable despair. Jesus wants you to rise up and walk! Take up that bed you may have been dragging around for years—which has identified you as an invalid and has been your source of security—and move on!

When feeling sorry for yourself has left you looking for a handout, throw up your hand and let Jesus pull you up. If you've been disabled or paralyzed by fear, kick those crutches to the curb and start stepping to the beat of a different drummer. Just keep in step with Jesus. When and if you experience a setback, don't worry; Jesus can turn every test into a testimony. He'll give you the power to get out of that pity party and start all over again.

Read About His Love

Jesus calls us to walk out of our pity party and into healing.

Read John 5: 1-9 and answer the questions below.

What were the diseases mentioned in verse 3?

How many years had the man been lying beside that pool?

What did Jesus ask him, and how did he respond?

What kind of healing do you need today?

How long have you sought healing?

What would it mean for you to get up and walk?

I want to share with you a psalm that calls us out of our self-pity and into praise. The psalmist proclaims praise for God's healing power and presence, and I want you to claim that power and presence in your life today.

Read Psalm 103:1-5 (CEB) and underline the words that stand out to you.

Let my whole being bless the LORD!
Let everything inside me
bless his holy name!
Let my whole being bless the LORD
and never forget all his good deeds:
how God forgives all your sins,
heals all your sickness,
saves your life from the pit,
crowns you with faithful love
and compassion,
and satisfies you
with plenty of good things
so that your youth
is made fresh like an eagle's.

Naming our blessings is one way of walking out of our self-pity. What are the "plenty of good things" in your life?

Pray About His Love

Friend, I don't know where this Scripture meets you today, but I want to pray a special prayer for healing in your life.

Dear healing, heavenly Father,
Thank You that You love us so much that You want us to be healed, to be made well. You love us so much that You would send a Healer not only to save us from our sins, but also to heal us from our sickness. Forgive us for sitting around and wallowing in our self-pity. Forgive us for making excuses. Forgive us for choosing to complain and stay comfortably in our brokenness when You have called us to get up and

walk into wellness. Make us stronger in the broken places. We want to be made well. We want to tell everyone we know the story of Your healing power in our lives. We love You, Lord. In Jesus' name, I pray. Amen.

Be About His Love

The subject of self-pity can be hard to face. We don't like to think that we make excuses for ourselves. Most of us probably wouldn't want to admit that we have been like that man by the pool with our list of excuses. Sometimes we're more comfortable in what we know instead of walking out of our pain and into a world of wholeness. So today, I want you to take a good look at yourself. What is your ailment? What are your excuses? Make a list of the excuses you have made for yourself about why you can't get to a place of healing. Then, cross them out one by one as you declare to Jesus that you do want to be healed!

DAY 4: MAKE A DIFFERENCE

"You are the salt of the earth; but if the salt loses its flavor how shall it be seasoned? It is then good for nothing but to be thrown out and trampled underfoot by men."
Matthew 5:13

Think About His Love

By His power, God has divinely "seasoned" you to make an amazing difference in this world for His glory. As a matter of fact, as a lover of the Lord Jesus, you add flavor to life and you make the Christian life appealing to others.

As a young girl, I watched my grandma in the kitchen, and I was amazed how she could put together a recipe without using measuring cups or measuring spoons. When making biscuits, for example, she would scoop some flour into a bowl with her hand, pour in some baking powder or baking soda, add a dash or two of salt, toss in some bacon fat or lard, and pour some buttermilk into the mixture. She would blend it all together, knead it briefly, roll it out, and then cut the dough with the rim of a coffee cup or mason jar. Then she would place the flat discs of dough on a greased pan, pop it in the oven, and presto—there in front of your eyes were golden-brown, light-as-a-feather biscuits.

Decades after Grandma died, I acquired a bread-making machine. I was determined to have a healthy diet despite the convenience of manufactured foods, which are full of preservatives and long lists of substances—the names of which I cannot pronounce. In my first attempts at bread making, I noticed the recipe called for 1 ½ teaspoons of salt. Because I understand that salt waterlogs tissues, robs calcium from the body, paralyzes the 260 taste buds in the mouth, is a heart poison, increases irritability of the nervous system, and is a leading cause of high blood pressure, I decided to eliminate salt from the bread recipe.

I dumped the ingredients, minus the salt, into the bread maker, pushed the buttons, and smiled. Within a short time, the yeasty smell of baking bread filled the house, and my mouth watered for the taste of a warm slice of buttered bread.

During the baking process I peeked at the loaf through the glass top of the machine and noticed that the loaf had risen magnificently. My excitement increased. The timer indicated that within the hour the bread would be ready. I had plenty of time to dash to the store to get some unsalted creamery butter and some strawberry preserves. Shortly after my return, the bread machine signaled that the baking process was complete.

When I raised the lid, to my dismay, I discovered that the loaf that had risen so majestically had fallen and had become a tough, gnarled lump. The color was golden, the taste was bearable, but the texture left a lot to be desired. I read the troubleshooting section of the owner's manual and discovered that the problem, most likely, was a lack of salt. A little salt can make a big difference.

God calls us to be "salt," to make a big difference in this world for Him. In Matthew 5, Jesus preached one of His greatest sermons, which we now refer to as the Sermon on the Mount. The message is revolutionary. Even today, it turns the world order upside down—first with a section we call the "Beatitudes," when Jesus began by saying, "Blessed are the poor in spirit, for theirs is the kingdom of heaven" (v. 3).

In Matthew 19:24 (NIV), Jesus told the disciples it would be easier for a camel to go through the eye of a needle than for a rich man to be saved. The next verse says they were "greatly astonished," asking Jesus, "Who then can be saved?" This is yet another example of how Jesus looked at the traditional wisdom and turned it inside out.

Jesus looked at the despised stations in life and called them "blessed." In the Sermon on the Mount, Jesus promised that those who mourn will be comforted, that the meek will inherit the earth, that those who hunger and thirst for righteousness will be filled, and that the merciful will obtain mercy (Matthew 5:4-7). Then He said this:

Blessed are you when they revile and persecute you, and say all kinds of evil against you falsely for my sake. Rejoice and be exceedingly glad, for great is your reward in heaven, for so they persecuted the prophets who were before you. You are the salt of the earth; but if the salt loses its flavor, how shall it be seasoned? It is then good for nothing but to be thrown out and trampled underfoot by men.

Matthew 5:11-13 NKJV

In a world filled with violence, hatred, selfishness, pride, deception, and greed, as blood-bought believers in Jesus Christ, we are called upon to season this unsavory mix. There is only one ingredient that can change this bitter brew, and it is the most important ingredient: love.

Years ago, early in my music ministry, I was invited to sing in Ft. Lauderdale, Florida. Until that time, Charles and I had been driving by car to our engagements that were, for the most part, no more than two to three hours from home. This trip would mark the first time we would board an airplane to travel to a concert date. We were extremely excited to be going to another state to share our music ministry.

Our host not only flew us to Ft. Lauderdale; he also sent a chauffeur-driven limousine to pick us up from the airport. Needless to say, Charles and I were simply beside ourselves when the driver ushered us to his long black limo. He swung open the door and motioned for us to step inside. Then he stored our bags in the massive trunk and took us on the scenic route to the hotel.

Our eyes widened like kids on Christmas morning as we took in all the luxurious scenes along the harbor. Gorgeous homes lined the shore while huge private yachts sailed the crystal blue ocean waters. Enjoying the view, Charles and I remarked to each other that we could really get used to this kind of treatment.

As the driver pulled onto the property where the luxury hotel was located, my eyes glanced up to the top of the tall skyscraper-like building where we'd be spending the night. I marveled at the meticulous landscaping that lined the drive.

It was then that I saw something out of the ordinary that is still etched in my memory right to this very moment. Nestled among the neatly trimmed shrubs was a homeless man, asleep on a cardboard box. I couldn't believe my eyes. This scene of the homeless man lying on a piece of cardboard juxtaposed to the high-rise luxury hotel full of nice, clean beds sent my head spinning. I felt a huge nudge from the Holy Spirit, giving me permission to enjoy the advantages I had been given, but never to get too comfortable.

After the car pulled up to the front door of the hotel, we walked over to where I had seen the man sleeping. Charles and I wanted to help in some way. We were even willing to offer him a room for the night, but the attendants had chased him off the property. We missed a chance to share God's love, but we learned something that day about our desire to make a difference. Christ has assigned to us, as believers in His name, the great task of adding love to this world's bitter mix. He has given us the mission of making the world a little bit more like heaven on earth. He calls us to make a big difference wherever we go and whatever situations we face. Our task is to keep our eyes open and to be bold as we reach out in His name.

> [God] calls us to make a big difference. . . . Our task is to keep our eyes open and to be bold as we reach out in His name.

Read About His Love

The Sermon on the Mount points us in the direction of how to make a big difference in the world. Let's see how Jesus' sermon speaks to our everyday lives even now.

Look in Matthew 5 (NIV) to complete the following sentences:

Blessed are the poor in spirit, for theirs is

_____ _____ ____

_____.

Blessed are those who mourn, for they will

_____ _____.

Blessed are the meek, for they _____

_____ _____

_____.

Blessed are those who hunger and thirst for

righteousness, for they _____ _____

_____.

Blessed are the merciful, for they will _____

_____ _____.

Blessed are the pure in heart, for they _____

_____ _____.

Blessed are the peacemakers, for they will be

called _____ _____

_____.

Blessed are those who are persecuted because of

righteousness, for theirs is _____

_____ _____.

_____.

Write verse 13 in your own words:

Now write verses 14-16 in your own words:

What do you think Jesus is saying in Matthew chapter 5? How does His teaching speak directly to your life today?

Pray About His Love

Let's pray together, my friend.

Lord, I come with this request
I'll not just ask for me today
But teach me how to love like Jesus
So that others may know the way

Use my words to be a comfort
To some lost and lonely soul
Show me how to shine in darkness
When the world is dark and cold

Fill me with a deep compassion
Less of me and more of You
May I never have to wonder
What on earth would Jesus do

Who will go and feed the hungry
Who'll take time to meet the need?
I know the answer to these questions
Here am I, Lord. Please send me

In Jesus' name. Amen.

"You are the salt of the earth. But if the salt loses its saltiness, how can it be made salty again? It is no longer good for anything, except to be thrown out and trampled under-foot." (Matthew 5:13 NIV)

Be About His Love

Remember, you are an ambassador of Christ. You are on display as you represent Jesus in your home, in the workplace, on the city bus, at the grocery store, on the expressway—wherever you go, the love of Christ goes with you. Will you make yourself available to be used by God today? Pray for a specific opportunity to represent Jesus in some way. Then pay attention…be on the lookout for God to send someone your way who needs your words, your kindness, or your mercy. After you make a big difference in someone's life today, make sure to give God the glory, and thank Him for empowering you to do it.

Agape—that highest and noblest form of love which sees something infinitely precious in its object.

DAY 5: THE POWER OF LOVE

He who does not love does not know God, for God is love.
1 John 4:8

Think About His Love

Today I want to start where we left off yesterday and go a little deeper into how it is that we make a difference in this world. I want us to look closely at the word *love* and what it means, because in our English language this small word has many meanings.

We love French fries and fast cars. We love our family and friends. We fall in love and we make love. In Greek, the language of the New Testament, there are four words to express that for which we have only one word in English:

Agape: affection or benevolence
Thelo: to delight in, desire, or be disposed toward
Phileo: to be a friend of[7]
Eros: to be sexually attracted to[8]

The *Tyndale New Bible Dictionary* gives the etymology of the word *agape* and defines it as "that highest and noblest form of love which sees something infinitely precious in its object."[9]

In 1 John 4:8 (NKJV) the writer says, "He who does not love does not know God, for God is love." When we come to fully understand this simple statement—"God is love"—we take hold of the eternal power that changes the world.

The world has yet to learn that love is more powerful than weapons of mass destruction. Warfare might change the landscape. War can even change behavior. But *love changes the heart.*

In His wonderful Sermon on the Mount, Jesus taught that we should love our enemies. He told us to pray for those who misuse us—a revolutionary idea then, when Israel was struggling under the iron rule of the Roman Empire. Now that the threat of terrorism causes us to walk barefooted through airport check points, we see that the power of love still has a lot to confront.

Love is a weapon that often goes untested during times of war. In spite of popular opinion, I have heard that the United States gives less than 1 percent of its budget to foreign aid, while military spending is 19 percent.[10] I wonder what would happen worldwide if we were to build schools, roads, and bridges; provide safe drinking water and sanitation; and feed the world's hungry instead of destroying millions of tons of food? I wonder what the global outcome would be if this nation was totally committed to being the salt of the earth?

Well, it's unlikely that United States foreign aid will ever equal the military budget; however, in the kingdom of God, love is the primary weapon of war. The power of love, intertwined with the gift of grace, dismisses all faults and guilt and gives a poor, desperate, and downcast world the hope it so desperately needs.

Within this framework, Jesus urges us to love one another so that the world will know we are His disciples. It is in this framework as well that John drew a sharp distinction between the words *agape* and *phileo* in Christ's conversation with Peter on the shores of the Sea of Tiberias.

Upon closer examination of John 21:15-17, we see Peter's willingness to use the words *phileo se* (I am your friend) rather than *agapo se* (I love you unconditionally). The *Tyndale New Bible Dictionary* says, "It is difficult to see why a writer of such simple Greek as John should have used two words in this context unless he intended a distinction be drawn between their meanings."[11]

It seems apparent that John, who was an eyewitness of that conversation between Peter and Jesus, simply records Peter's reluctance to make an unconditional commitment. When the Lord asked, "Do you love me?" Peter answered, "I am your friend." (Remember that Peter was talking to the risen Christ, who had demonstrated to the fullest extent His *agape* love for all humanity at Calvary some forty days earlier. He had done so in spite of unbelievable humiliation, degradation, horrendous torture, and death.)

Now, our Lord was standing as Love personified, asking Peter for a full commitment in response to the love He had extended. His admonition to Peter to "feed my sheep" was a direct instruction for him to make a big difference in this world through the power of love. The word of God sets the standard for us to love one another today—whether it is by teaching the word (as it was in Peter's case) or just lending a helping hand to someone in need. Our heavenly Father admonishes us to share His love with everyone we meet.

155

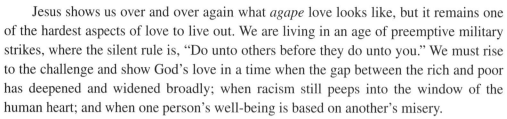

Jesus shows us over and over again what *agape* love looks like, but it remains one of the hardest aspects of love to live out. We are living in an age of preemptive military strikes, where the silent rule is, "Do unto others before they do unto you." We must rise to the challenge and show God's love in a time when the gap between the rich and poor has deepened and widened broadly; when racism still peeps into the window of the human heart; and when one person's well-being is based on another's misery.

Christ tells us that as we journey through this life in our day-to-day experiences (and we don't have to go out of our way, by the way), we can embrace someone who has suffered an attack from the enemy. We can take time from our busy schedules to become actively involved in the welfare of our neighbor. We can show concern. We can speak kind words. We can commit our resources. We can "go" into the harvest field, or we can "send" someone else.

We can express real, *agape* love to another person who, like us, has been created in the image of God. And that image is Love.

And you know what I have learned along the way? In the same way that a little bit of salt can go a long way, a little bit of love goes a long, long way.

Often, it's the little things that count the most. Call the widow down the street and take her grocery list with you when you go shopping. Call the single mom who is working two jobs and tell her you'd like for her kids to come over for pizza with yours. When you've cranked up your snow blower to clear your sidewalk, don't stop at the property line. When you've harvested your vegetable garden and eaten all you can, and canned all you can't eat, call your neighbors across the street and offer them some vegetables.

Showing love is not complicated. My Grandma said when she lived as a sharecropper in the Deep South that she never knew of the Great Depression until she heard about it on the radio. The family lived on a river, and Grandpa caught fish and kept them alive (in the river) in a big wood-framed box covered with fence wire. They had a vegetable garden and some chickens. One of their neighbors had a milk cow, and another neighbor had hogs; another raised sugar cane and molasses.

When Grandma needed butter, she'd tell one of the kids, "Take Miss Sally a dozen eggs and tell her to send me some butter." Sometimes a neighbor would send some lard, bacon, or ham in exchange for some fish. Coffee, flour, and cornmeal largely comprised the shopping list because they lived in community and because they loved one another.

Those country folks not only understood what real *agape* love was all about; they truly lived out the principles of the Scriptures. In their own simple way, they showed the world how to love in the true meaning of the word.

Not long ago I heard someone say, "There's so much trouble in the world. Somebody needs to do something." Oftentimes we feel helpless to effect change in this great big world of ours, and we feel that our "little bit" makes no difference. However, the words of the English author and Anglican cleric Sydney Smith reveal what is actually true: "It is the greatest of all mistakes to do nothing because you can only do a little. Do what you can."[12]

Doing what you can while seasoning your actions with the love of Christ is the greatest gift of all. It's never too late to show real love.

Read About His Love

Today I have covered or pointed to a lot of precious Scripture gems. Now I want you to go through each of the passages; slow down and reread where needed, and be sensitive to the leading of the Holy Spirit. Write what each passage reveals to you about *agape* love.

1 John 4:8

Matthew 5:44

John 17:20-23

John 21:15-17

Matthew 5:41

Romans 12:19-20

Luke 10:25b-37

1 John 4:7-8

Pray About His Love

Let's call upon Paul's prayer for the church at Ephesus in Ephesians 3:14-21 (NKJV) and make it our prayer for one another:

I bow my knees to the Father of our Lord Jesus Christ, from whom the whole family in heaven and earth is named, that He would grant you, according to the riches of His glory, to be strengthened with might through His Spirit in the inner man, that Christ may dwell in your hearts through faith; that you, being rooted and grounded in love, may be able to comprehend with all the saints what is the width and length and depth and height—to know the love of Christ which passes knowledge; that you may be filled with all the fullness of God. Now to Him who is able to do exceedingly abundantly above all that we ask or think, according to the power that works in us, to Him be glory in the church by Christ Jesus to all generations, forever and ever. Amen.

Be About His Love

What has the Lord quickened in your heart today? How easy is it for you to demonstrate *agape* love to others? Where have you had trouble showing love? Make a list of the things that keep you from unconditional love and ask God to grant you more love and more freedom to share His love freely.

VIDEO VIEWER GUIDE

Promise 6: You have the ability to accomplish _____ _____ in God's name.

_____ out.

F   _____

A   _____

I   _____

T   _____

H   _____

_____ up.

Only by stepping out and rising up do you _____ yourself to make a

_____ _____ in the world.

Now unto him that is able to do _____ abundantly above all

that we ask or think, according to the _____ that works in us.

Ephesians 3:20 King James 2000

Week 7

You Are Equipped With Unique Gifts and Talents

God has equipped each of us with gifts and talents to accomplish His specific will and purpose for our lives with ease. There's nothing more fulfilling than traveling in the lane where you know you are assigned. When you are confident of God's call on your life, you will not be concerned about the gifts and talents of others. What I've said before bears repeating. You will not be jealous or envious of their success, comparing yourself to them. Rather, you will find that you can celebrate them, instead.

Over the next several days we will pump up the volume on your life assignment. God's promise within you is limitless, boundless, and inexhaustible. It's running over with power according to Ephesians 3:20, which we prayed together at the end of Week 6. As you walk in your assignment, my friend, God will do "exceeding abundantly above" your greatest dreams, according to His mighty power that is at work within you.

Just as a cook stirs a wonderful pot of flavorful homemade soup that's been simmering on low heat atop the back burner of the stove, the Lord desires to reach down to the bottom of your heart and stir your gifts from the bottom up, releasing all of your Godlike potential.

Today, I want you to think on these beautiful things: *Because God loves me, He has bestowed upon me gifts and talents to use for His glory. I will make myself available to Him.*

Scripture Memorization

Throughout the week, continue focusing on our memory verse, John 17:23 (NCV):

"I will be in them and you will be in me so that they will be completely one. Then the world will know that you sent me and that you loved them just as much as you loved me."

Continue using the index cards in visible places and reading the verse when you get up, throughout the day, and as you go to bed. Remember that another great way to memorize Scripture is to write or type it.

DAY 1: ENCOURAGE YOUR HEART

But David encouraged himself in the LORD his God.
1 Samuel 30:6 KJV

Think About His Love

The task can never be too hard, or times too tough, for you to encourage yourself in God.

Have you ever been faced with so much discouragement that your only response was to cry? I don't mean you responded with a whimper or a whine. I mean, has your heart ever been so broken that your only outlet was to wail with grief? I know this feeling of uncontrolled sadness all too well.

One weekend I had the privilege of speaking to a wonderful group of ladies at a beautiful Mother's Day brunch in the state of Texas. As the event was ending, I made my way to my product table where I could enjoy some time to meet the ladies who had attended the event. This is the best part for me—meeting ladies person to person, praying with them and hearing a brief part of their stories. One beautiful, well-dressed lady stepped up in the line. She could barely get her words out before she began to cry. The tears welled up in her eyes as she choked out the words between her tears. She told me that her husband had taken his own life just a few weeks before, and she was left with so many questions, the pain and suffering of living as a widow, and the endless days and nights of unresolved grief. I could sense this dear woman's deepest pain. Although I'd never walked that road before, I felt her grief right down to the depths of my soul.

I prayed for her while she held on to me as if for dear life. We cried and cried many tears as we mourned the loss of a husband and friend gone way too soon. After we finished praying and crying, she gathered herself and stepped aside. I promised to be praying for her.

Next, a young lady stepped up and took me by the hand. She said, "That was my mother." Immediately, I felt the pangs of grief gnawing at my heart all over again as I sensed the heartache this young lady must have been experiencing over the loss of her father and the need to be strength for her mother during this dark season of their lives. I could see that, on the outside, this beautiful young woman had a resolve of pure iron, but underneath her heart was crumbling under the stress of having to be the one her mother leaned on. Again, I wept deep, silent sobs of grief for this dear family as I prayed with this sweet daughter. I don't know when I have felt so much pain for two strangers. But in a sense, we were not strangers at all. We were sisters overcome by the weight of life's circumstances, facing the uncertainty of the future while trusting God who knows just what lies ahead.

King David was familiar with this kind of deep, gnawing grief. I want to share with you an insight I discovered from his life. First Samuel 30:1-6 tells us that David and his troops came home to Ziklag, only to find everything they held dear completely wiped out. The wicked Amalekites had raided the town, setting it on fire. Then they took the women and children and everyone else, young and old alike, as their prisoners. When David and his soldiers returned to find their homes smoldering in ruins and all of their loved ones gone, the Bible says these mighty men wept until they had no more power to weep.

The word *discouragement* does not begin to describe the condition of David and his men. As their leader, David even had to endure the threat of his own troops turning against him in the wake of this horrendous mess. In spite of it all, the Bible tells us that "David encouraged himself in the LORD his God" (1 Samuel 30:6 KJV).

There was no one around who would—or even could—encourage David at this point. So, David did for himself what no one else could do for him.

Do you have deep disappointments that weigh heavily in your heart? Have your hopes and dreams literally gone up in smoke? Are you feeling the deep pain and sting of suffering a great loss? Take comfort, my friend. You don't have to wait for others to speak the encouraging words you long to hear. You can speak over yourself like David did— *encourage yourself in the Lord your God.*

How do you begin? Keep reading, dear one. Soon you will be filling your own heart with the encouragement you need.

Because we are spiritual beings who are engaged in spiritual warfare, the enemy's priority is to wound or kill our spirit. Sadly, he is increasingly successful in the world today. At various times in our lives, we can all experience episodes of stress, unhappiness, sadness, or grief. Often when we suffer a personal tragedy like the loss of a loved one, a severe difficulty like a divorce, or the loss of a job, we may feel deeply depressed. Most of us are able to deal with these kinds of situations in a productive way.

Clinical depression, however, goes far beyond the experience of grief or a feeling of sadness. This illness can challenge your ability to perform even routine daily activities. In the extreme, depression may even lead to suicide. I have read that clinical depression is among the fastest growing mental illnesses in our nation. It affects people of every race, age, gender, and income level, regardless of their religious background. As a result, the use of antidepressants is widely on the rise, and support groups and various therapies abound— but the number of depressed individuals continues to grow.[13]

So what is the solution for us and for the millions who are suffering under this yoke of oppression? Let's go back to David a moment. In 1 Samuel 29, just before David and his men returned to find Ziklag spoiled by the Amalekites, another enemy of Israel, the Philistines, remembered God's favor upon David's life (vv. 3, 5).

Just like a child rehearses her ABCs or multiplication tables until she knows them "by heart," rehearse the promises of God until they bring your heart the peace that passes all understanding.

My point is this: as God brings you to center stage, tapping your gifts and abilities and using you to advance His kingdom, stay on the alert. Watch and pray because the enemy can recognize God's hand upon your life; he'll do whatever he can to wound you and stall your progress.

But God . . ., my sister! But God is faithful. Our enemy, the devil, is a liar and a defeated foe. Though he may attack us by stealth, doing his best to hit us hard and unexpectedly, hoping his wicked scheme of discouragement and depression will pull us under, *we only need to stand in faith and remember*—God has already gone before us and paved the way to victory. Father God is working *all things together* for our good—*because we love Him* and are "called according to His purpose" (Romans 8:28 KJV).

Sometimes, by choice or by design, there may come a time in your life when there will be no encourager to physically comfort you or lift you up with edifying words. There may be no cheerleader to rally you on. There may be no preacher to motivate you and no choir to lead you in a song of praise.

When the dark night of the soul has stolen your hopes and dashed your dreams and the pain of life drives you into your prayer closet, cry out to God—even if you've already cried until you think you can cry no more. Take all the time you need in that solitary place. While you are there, talk to God and listen to Him. Allow Him to have the last word concerning your situation. When you come out, talk to yourself; meditate about everything God has said and shown you in His word.

When you have given your situation fully over to God, you will emerge much stronger, remembering that situations and circumstances may change with the weather but the God you serve never changes. Just like a child rehearses her ABCs or multiplication tables until she knows them "by heart," rehearse the promises of God until they bring your heart the peace that passes all understanding. Take what God has said to you at face value, knowing that no one can encourage you the way you can encourage yourself.

Read About His Love

The ability to encourage yourself is a precious gift from God. Think about how His boundless love for you is so great that He made a way for you to remind yourself of His power within you and receive help directly from Him just when you need it most.

Read 1 Samuel 30:1-6. Make a list of the terrible things that David faced as he returned to Ziklag.

What words would you use to describe his situation?

When you read the words "David encouraged Himself in the Lord," what kind of encouraging words and thoughts do you think might have come to his mind?

When have you felt like you were completely alone, standing right in the middle of despair? How did you make it out of that despairing place?

Flip through the Book of Psalms, looking for psalms that begin with words of despair but end with encouraging words of hope and praise. Write below the references for the psalms and verses that speak to you. Highlight or mark them in your Bible as a reference for times when you need to encourage yourself.

Pray About His Love

Let's pause and thank God, who encourages us:

Dear heavenly Father,

It is with great humility that I approach Your throne. I thank You, dear Father, that I can find everything I need in You. My friends and loved ones are indeed a blessing. I am much richer because they are in my life. But when they leave and go home, they do not leave me lonely... because You are still with me. Even in my lowest moments, during seasons of my greatest loss, thank You, Lord, that I need not look to anyone but You to supply my deepest need for encouragement. Please help me to meditate on Your word instead of my circumstances. Today, as I encourage myself, meditating on Your promises, I will be ever mindful of Your great love for me. In Jesus' name. Amen.

Be About His Love

How can you practice the habit of encouraging yourself this week? Jot down an example in the space below, or consider recording your thoughts in the journaling pages

in this book or your own journal. Your entry might look something like this: Instead of speaking negative words about my weight, I will encourage myself with the truth that God says I'm beautiful. He will help me make better choices concerning the things I eat. According to Philippians 4:13, "I can do all things through Christ who strengthens me" (NKJV).

> I can do all things through Christ who strengthens me. (Philippians 4:13 NKJV)

DAY 2: LOOK FOR GOD

The joy of the LORD is your strength.
Nehemiah 8:10 KJV

Think About His Love

Yesterday we learned that David *encouraged himself in the Lord* when he faced utter despair, tremendous loss, and certain loneliness. Today, I want us to look at some tools that will help us encourage ourselves when we can't see a way out of the mire and the messes of life.

In Psalm 137, God's people, the children of Judah, had been released from Babylonian captivity. Yet they recalled the horrific and depressing experience they encountered at the hands of their captors. They remembered the enemy's taunting requests to "sing us one of the songs of Zion" (v. 3b KJV). In the next verse, God's heart-broken people responded rhetorically: "How shall we sing the LORD's song in a strange land?" In other words, "How can we sing at a time like this?" It was a time of national spiritual depression.

Likewise, Jesus' stunned disciples must have felt overwhelming sadness, confusion, and fear on that day when His mutilated body was laid in the tomb. This was no time for gaiety or even the consideration of future endeavors; there was only a sense of intense hopelessness. This brings to my mind the conditions that gave birth to the Negro spiritual, which was conceived in oppression, hatred, degradation, and estrangement, yet has become a powerful genre that brings glory to God.

You see, God has placed a harp deep within the human soul. Even though you may not be able to carry a tune or play an instrument, the harp in your soul is an instrument of joy, lightheartedness, and true worship. In every circumstance, as you call upon God and lift up your heavenly instrument in praise, it will carry you into His presence. This harp in you can even take a mournful tune and bring encouragement to a severely downcast soul.

A song with such a soul-stirring melody comes readily to mind; it was written by Clara Ward. I remember it best as it was sung by the late, great Mahalia Jackson. It simply says, "And my soul look[ed] back and wonder[ed] how I got over."[14] Even when remembering difficult times, you can encourage yourself by looking back and reviewing your history with God. Regardless of the circumstance, you will find that God has a perfect track record. Truly, He cannot, and will not, fail you.

To encourage ourselves, sometimes we need to look back to see what God has done. As you look back over your life, consider just for a moment the things God has brought you through. As you do this, don't focus on the battles and setbacks that life has caused but on the victories that God has won for you. Doesn't it do your heart good to remember God's faithfulness and goodness to you, even in the midst of life's challenges?

Recently, I had a phone conversation with a young lady whom God has delivered from drug addiction. She is currently struggling with spousal infidelity, but still she seemed quite excited about the new life she has found in Christ.

I asked rather tentatively why her husband's infidelity didn't seem to bother her very much. She said, "Oh, yes, it bothers me a lot; but when I think about how God took me off drugs cold turkey…no counseling, no twelve-step program, no gradual withdrawal—and I had used drugs since I was fourteen years old and now I'm twenty-eight—I realize this is trying to pull me back into that world of addiction and violence. But I know if God can deliver me from drugs, cold turkey, with no side effects, there ain't nothing God can't do. So, even if my marriage seems doomed, even if my husband leaves me for another woman, even if I am struggling to forgive his infidelity, I know if God can do all of these things for me, then I know that He can give me the strength I need to be victorious in this too."

I listened to this new believer who was baptized only a few months ago, the mother of three beautiful children, whose marriage is under severe attack. I listened to her praising God for what He has brought her through, in spite of the situation she is currently facing. When I hung up the phone, I felt a shout coming on and said, "You go, God!" Then I began to reflect on the storms God has brought me through, and my spirit soared in worship. I sat right there at my desk and had church all by myself!

We can also encourage ourselves sometimes by looking inward to see what God has to teach us, how He is trying to change us, and how He is attempting to mold us into the image of His Son. Introspection can be a difficult process because the image we see in the mirror usually looks pretty good from our own biased perspective. It is much easier to see the faults of others than our own. Before we can fully enjoy the benefits of lifting up our own countenance, we must first recognize the problem that has brought us down.

I know a Christian couple who began dating last year. She is an accountant, and he is a journalist. He is a wordsmith and she is a number cruncher. Her language skills are not as sharp as his, and he is more concerned with the analytical process than getting to the bottom line. She told me they both love the Lord and believe that God ordered their steps to meet, but their personality differences and their personal idiosyncrasies (which may seem small and insignificant to others) kept them at odds.

In their casual conversations, she felt as if each sentence she uttered was being scrutinized. He'd often ask, "What do you mean by that statement?" And she would rephrase her thoughts, trying to clarify an intended meaning. Then he would retort, "But that's not what you said originally. Why don't you say what you mean?" Conversely, he took great pains to give a detailed explanation to what she considered to be simple and practical questions. She found herself tuning him out or telling him, "Why don't you just get to the point?"

Their fragile relationship was on the verge of being fatally fractured, although they claimed to love each other deeply. Then one Sunday morning as they sat together in church listening to the pastor's sermon, he spoke of God's grace extended through His love for humanity. The conclusion of the sermon was that God's desire is for believers to extend grace to one another.

My friend told me that as the pastor concluded the message, she and her boyfriend, without saying a word, looked at each other with tear-streaked cheeks, strongly convicted of their lack of grace toward each other. After hearing the message, instead of pointing an accusing finger at each other, they saw themselves reflected in the words of Scripture.

Perhaps the greatest obstacle to introspection is getting over the notion that we are without fault. Once we overcome that obstacle, however, it is greatly encouraging to take a look at what God wants us to become. How valuable it is to understand that little by little, God is bringing us, often kicking and screaming, to a place of great joy and completeness.

Another way of encouraging ourselves is to look around to see the ways God is moving in the world around you. One of my students in the college songwriting class I teach is a young single mother. She is often stretched and stressed by working, going to school, and taking care of her pre-school-aged daughter. One day after class, she stayed behind and openly shared her challenges with me:

It was an idyllic morning in early March . . . and the earth was responding with new growth and bird songs. I had dropped off my four-year-old at pre-school after one of those mornings when it seemed nothing was going right. . . . It was a morning when I had forgotten to put coffee on the grocery list and there wasn't even enough for one full cup, so I skipped coffee. It was a morning when I had washed a load of clothes, then discovered, after the fact, that water temperature had been inadvertently turned to "hot," and before I finished my morning shower, the water ran cold.

It was a morning when one of the tires on the car looked low and when I drove to the gas station to put some air in the "soft" tire, I heard the telltale hissing sound of my car's right front tire going flat. What a way to start the day! It was one of those mornings when you feel you should have just stayed in bed.

But then it happened. On the return trip from pre-school, I was heading east with the morning sun. It was not quite high enough for the car's visor to block it out. It was nearly blinding my vision when I stopped at a red light. I was full of attitude by now, even disgusted with the morning sun that caused me to squint at the traffic light. . . .

Then I noticed this person in the cross-walk. It was a young guy, maybe in his mid-twenties. Apparently he was afflicted with muscular dystrophy because he laboriously made his way across the street using two crutch-like appliances, half-dragging his lower torso along. Then I looked more closely and saw on his face a grin that stretched from ear to ear, as his head wobbled loosely with his stumbling gait. What a smile!

He wasn't grinning at me. He didn't even look in my direction. His countenance reflected the pure joy of living. And there I sat in my car grumbling over a lack of coffee, a lukewarm shower, a soft tire, and sunshine in my face. The Holy Spirit convicted me immediately. I was not walking, although I was perfectly capable. No, I was riding in an automobile, which (although it was not new) was paid for, and (although it had a leaky tire) I had money enough to get it repaired.

Not only had I dressed myself this morning, but my four-year-old as well; and I was not struggling alone on my journey through life, but had the joy of parenting a young child. And finally, I realized that the same sunshine that had caused me to squint and complain brought hilarity to this person, to whom life had dealt a much tougher hand.

I marveled at what I had just witnessed. A car behind me honked. The light had turned green. God had used a complete stranger, but a fellow traveler, to save me from a day of discouragement, and some days later, there are moments when I still see that infections grinning face.

Quite frankly, I haven't had a bad morning since. Many times, we can encourage ourselves by simply looking around. Usually, I don't have to look any farther than my own front door to know how blessed I am. I simply need to look around.

Finally, we encourage ourselves by meditating on the promises of God. When you meditate on God's Word, you are reminding yourself of what you know to be true about God.

Whether you are walking down a hallway to an appointment, standing in line at the Department of Motor Vehicles, or sitting down to catch a nap, keeping your mind on the Lord will cause you to be encouraged, productive, and fruitful. Discouragement will tell you that the whole world is against you and that nothing is going to work out. Encouragement, on the other hand, will tell you that Jesus, who is always on your side, is much greater than a whole world against you.

Oh yes! Even when the fallout of warfare is all around you, and even if no one is standing with you, God has made a way. You can encourage yourself in the LORD, just like David did, because "the joy of the LORD" is your strength" (Nehemiah 8:10 NIV).

Read About His Love

To encourage ourselves in the Lord, we need to remember what God has done in the past, look inward to see what God has to teach us, look outward to see how God is moving in the world around us, and look to God's Word for His promises of faithfulness.

Read 2 Corinthians 4:8-9. Notice the despair and the hope in each line and record it below:

We are _____ but

not_____;

_____ but not

_____;

_____ but not

_____;

_____but not

_____.

When have you felt "pressed on every side" (NIV)?

How did you hold onto hope that you would not be "crushed"? (NIV)

Look up these powerful passages from God's Word to remind you just how big God is, so you'll always remember—even in the midnight hour—both who and whose you are:

1 Peter 2:9   **You are part of a** _____.

John 13:35	You are one of Jesus' _____.
John 15:14	You are Jesus' _____.
Isaiah 49:16	You are engraved on the palms of God's _____.
Matthew 5:13	You are the _____.
Matthew 5:14	You are the _____.
Romans 8:37	We are _____.
Numbers 13:30	We are able to _____.

The name of the LORD is a strong tower; The righteous run to it and are safe.
(Proverbs 18:10 NKJV)

Pray About His Love

Would you pray with me?

Dear heavenly Father,
*   My heart is so uplifted by Your word today. You have taught me that everything I will ever need is available in You. I admit, I have looked to others to encourage me with their words. But nothing can compare to the power of Your words! Even in times of great despair, I recall promises such as Proverbs 18:10: "The name of the LORD is a strong tower; The righteous run to it and are safe" (NKJV). How can I be discouraged with promises like these? When friends are nowhere to be found, help me not to wonder why. You bring Your Holy Word to my remembrance and my heart is carried away with praise. For this, I am most grateful. In Jesus' name I pray. Amen.*

Be About His Love

Experience God today by looking back to see what God has done in your life, by looking inward to see what God is teaching you, by looking outward to see how God is

moving around you, or by meditating on His promises all day long. Choose one way to encourage yourself and practice it today. Write a few notes about how the experience gave you encouragement and hope, and develop these notes into a journal entry later.

DAY 3: EQUIP YOUR HANDS

By faith Moses' parents hid him for three months after he was born, because they saw he was no ordinary child, and they were not afraid of the king's edict.
Hebrews 11:23 NIV

Think About His Love

God has enabled us to accomplish great things. God loves you so much and has lavishly given you gifts and talents to do great things in His name. You are His masterpiece, pregnant with incredible promise to effect change in the world around you. There is also great promise in you for personal growth and change. With each passing day as you linger in God's embrace, you can become a better version of the person you were yesterday. I once met a lady during the break at a conference where I was speaking. At the session just prior to meeting her, I had been teaching about how important it is for us not to worry. She said to me, "I've always been a worrier. My mother was a worrier. My grandmother was a worrier too. I guess I'll always be a worrier."

Before I could chime in, another lady standing nearby added her insight. She said, "If you had a broken toe and had to walk on crutches, you wouldn't be satisfied to walk on crutches for the rest of your life, would you? No! You'd get that toe fixed! You can get that worry problem fixed too!" All I could do was laugh and add, "Amen, sister!"

Sweet friend, "We are more than conquerors through him who loved us" (Romans 8:37 NKJV). We never have to succumb to feelings of helplessness or remain stuck in life's dead-end situations. Jesus always offers us a better way. Whoever says that we can't grow and change is simply not telling the gospel truth.

In fact, as believers who aspire to become more and more like Jesus Christ, we must never stop growing toward excellence. Becoming who Christ has called us to be is our life's goal. We must take hold of His promises and live out the promise within us. If you are doing anything less than your absolute best for the cause of Christ, it is mediocrity.

Over the next two days, I want us to look at one such woman who was not satisfied with the way things were: Jochebed. As God would have it, her name means "Jehovahgloried."[15] Certainly Jochebed's life was a demonstration of God's glory, for she is highly esteemed as one of the greatest mothers in the Bible. Having possessed commendable character traits as a godly woman, she and her husband (Moses' parents) hold a well-deserved place of prominence in God's divine Hall of Faith in Hebrews 11:23.

God equipped this woman with great wisdom, courage, complete trust in Him, a dedication to her family, and a heart of total selflessness. These admirable qualities would alter the course of the entire Israelite nation. Because she stood on God's promise, the entire nation rose to greatness, in spite of a wicked pharaoh's edict to annihilate them.

Jochedbed's story begins in Exodus 1:22. To control the population, Pharaoh ordered that all newborn Hebrew boys be murdered. It was into this situation that Moses was born. With the help of her husband and two older children, Jochebed kept her little baby boy hidden for three months. Can you imagine how difficult it must have been for this mother to keep her baby hidden in the house? Surely, her newborn son (whom Pharaoh's daughter ultimately named Moses) cried as heartily as any other baby. No doubt, Jochebed kept all windows and doors tightly shut, even in what might have been sweltering heat, for fear that his cries would be heard by a nosy neighbor and her secret be exposed.

In my mind's eye, I can see her panic-stricken face with every knock at the door. As baby Moses grew, it likely became increasingly difficult to keep him hidden. With her back against the wall, Jochebed faced a very difficult decision.

Has your back ever been against the wall? Have you ever stood toe-to-toe with the difficult task of having to make an excruciating life-or-death decision? We will turn to Jochebed to see how God equipped her to stand strong in the face of a compromising culture.

It's interesting how many similarities there are between that culture and ours. Just as God called a woman named Jochebed into the spotlight, He is moving you out of the shadows of the backstage to play a big role in your life. So, let's see what you can glean from this great woman of God.

First of all, you must decide to obey God. Pharaoh's orders were clear. Throw all Hebrew baby boys into the Nile River. There is no telling how many mothers' hearts were shattered and how many newborn boys lost their lives to this dastardly order. Jochebed refused to obey this wicked order from this evil leader. She chose to obey God.

Confronted by this difficult decision, Moses' mother did an unusual thing. (And I don't think Jochebed came by this idea on her own.) She got an idea to put her baby in a wicker basket and place him among the reeds of the dangerous, crocodile-ridden River Nile. This idea did not originate from anywhere in this world, my friend. It was divinely inspired by God.

To any mother, this drastic decision would seem totally ridiculous. However, God in His divine design knew exactly what He was doing. It is obvious to me that Jochebed did what *she knew* God instructed her to do. Above every heart-wrenching circumstance she

Obedience is a key tool in equipping yourself for the work God has set out in advance for you to do.

faced, this brave woman obeyed God. Then she trusted Him to handle the rest. Isn't that the epitome of obedience?

You must do the same. When the enemy tries to put you in a chokehold, seek God and do what He tells you to do, regardless of how unconventional His instructions may be. Then leave the rest to Him. God will complete His plan, doing what only He can do.

In 1984 when my growing concert calendar began to compete with my middle school teaching job, common sense said, "Hang on to the job." My practical head knowledge reminded me that my husband had recently quit his job to start a new business. The pressures of meeting the needs of our growing family tempted me to rely on the security of my paycheck, as well as the healthcare and retirement benefits the school system provided.

For a solid year, I nursed a newborn and mothered another active elementary school-age son. I taught private piano and voice lessons. I held down my teaching job. I tried to keep up with a growing music ministry. Is it any wonder that I almost collapsed from exhaustion in the process? Of course, my husband did all those things that great fathers do. But there are some things that only a mother can accomplish.

I sought God with all my heart. He led me to follow Him, step off the conventional path, and trust Him for the rest. After I quit my job, I found that He provided everything we needed. All of our family's needs were gloriously met. The bills got paid. God even sent someone to contribute enough money for health care for the first year of our new music ministry.

Now, after pursuing this calling for more than half my life, I can truly say there is nothing more fulfilling than doing what I firmly believed God had called me to do. I can honestly share that I love what I do and I do what I love. Someone said if you love what you do, you'll never work a day in your life. Amen! Truly, God is faithful!

Remember that obedience is a key tool in equipping yourself for the work God has set out in advance for you to do. Whatever situation you find yourself in, seek obedience. Trust in the promises of God, who has called you and who will fully equip you for the journey.

Read About His Love

Let's compare Jochedbed's story with two other women in the Bible who also were equipped for significant moments—not just in their lives, but in all of history. They obeyed God, even when the situation seemed too much to bear.

1) Jochedbed
Read Exodus 1-2:10 and make a timeline of the events relayed in these verses to get a clear grasp on the details of the story.

In what ways do you see Jochebed's obedience to God and trust in God?

2) Esther
Let's look at another brave woman. Read Esther 4:12-17. What situation did Esther find herself in?

Look for the turning point in Esther's reaction, when she determined to act on behalf of God's people. What did she say?

3) Mary, the Mother of Jesus
Now let's look at Mary, the mother of Jesus. Read Luke 2:1-38. How did Mary respond to the angel Gabriel?

What did Mary say when she decided to obey God's call for her life?

These three women show us in different ways how God places us in certain situations and equips us to demonstrate His power when He calls on us, ultimately bringing Him glory. These women obeyed God even in trying circumstances. My prayer for us is that we will allow God to equip us for the task before us by first obeying His instructions every step of the way.

Pray About His Love

Let's pray together:

Dear heavenly Father,
   You are so awesome and mighty indeed! You have chosen us, loved us, and called us to certain times and places to bring You glory. We know that You will not call us to go where You are not. You will not leave us in the middle of nowhere to find our way home by ourselves. No, You love us enough to give us instructions. You love us enough to give us wisdom. You love us enough to give us a memory of all that You

have done before. You love us enough to give us Your Word that shows us in writing just how faithful You are. Thank you, Lord. Help us to be obedient when You call us to use our abilities, our gifts, and our talents. We will give You all the praise and glory. In Jesus' name. Amen.

Be About His Love

Today, spend some time reflecting on how you can use your gifts, talents, and abilities in your life right now. What is going on around you that you might have a special calling to help with, work on, or pray for? When you think of something, jot it down below and ask God to give you clear instructions; then practice obedience as you put your gifts to work for God. As you have time, record your thoughts and God's instructions in the journaling pages in this book or your own journal.

DAY 4: DEPEND ON GOD

Whatever you do, work at it with all your heart, as working for the Lord, not for men, since you know that you will receive an inheritance from the Lord as a reward. It is the Lord Christ you are serving.
Colossians 3:23-24 NIV

Think About His Love

Yesterday we looked at Jochebed's obedience as God equipped her for the awesome task before her. Today, we'll look at how important it is to depend on God when we face those touch-and-go situations.

To equip yourself for the days ahead, you must depend on God. Jochebed loved her baby, and he grew until he could no longer be kept a secret. Exodus 2:3 reveals that she had to resort to a drastic measure to save her child. She did what many mothers since then have had to do in order to save the lives of their babies—she gave her cherished child away. Oh, the anxiety she must have felt in her heart! With no idea where or how the baby would end up, Jochebed had to do an excruciatingly difficult thing. Only God could have helped this obedient woman carry out such a difficult task.

Some people think you must come to the place where you have complete and total peace before acting on a decision. I believe Moses' dear mother must have had many second thoughts before releasing her baby to what appeared to be an unknown fate. But again, it occurs to me that nothing ever "occurs" to God.

For this reason, we can do nothing in and of our own strength. *Like Jochebed, we are able to do what we are called to do, when we are commanded to do it, solely because God empowers us to do it.*

I am reminded of a passage I taught my children to memorize, so they could bring it to mind when facing times of difficulty. I recommend it to you today. It is found in Isaiah 41:10 (NKJV):

> *Fear not, for I am with you;*
> *Be not dismayed, for I am your God.*
> *I will strengthen you,*
> *Yes, I will help you,*
> *I will uphold you with My righteous right hand.*

As you depend on God, you also must uphold godly values. You must care about the things God cares about. The principles of honoring one's faith and family shine through like brilliant stars in Jochebed's God-story. The evidence that she loved the things God loves was reflected in the lives of her amazing children. Aaron became the first high priest of the nation of Israel. Miriam was a gifted poet, musician, and lead worshiper. Moses, the deliverer of the Israelites, became one of the greatest leaders the world has ever known. What a legacy this woman produced!

Even at the beginning of the story, when Miriam was around age ten, she already was much like her mother. Although she was young and maybe a bit naïve, she exhibited great godly wisdom when suggesting that her own mother be the one to nurse little Moses, after Pharaoh's daughter discovered her baby brother in the river.

It is clear that Jochebed placed her faith and family first. It is clear, as well, that her children followed in her footsteps. Many years later, God would equip Moses to lead the Hebrew nation out of Egypt. He would equip Aaron to be an eloquent spokesperson for Moses and their people, and He would equip Miriam to bless and encourage the Israelites just when they needed it most. Surely, God's promise in each of them proved to be incomparable.

So, what has God uniquely equipped you to do? If challenging the laws of an evil national leader or leading a nation out from the bonds of slavery seems way over your head, not to worry. As we have discussed on numerous occasions, God has a unique assignment for you. This call upon your life is something you were born to do. If you know what that assignment is, don't let fear, pride, pretense, or a need for approval get in your way. Rather, remember the Apostle Paul's encouraging words:

> *Whatever you do, work at it with all your heart, as working for the Lord, not for men, since you know that you will receive an inheritance from the Lord as a reward. It is the Lord Christ you are serving.*
>
> Colossians 3:23-24 NIV

God has a unique assignment for you. This call upon your life is something you were born to do.

177

You can accomplish great things for Christ because He has empowered you to do what He's called you to do. Your attitude as His child and willing servant should be one not of pressure or obligation, but of privilege. True servants don't say with dread, "Ugh! I have to do this." Instead, they say with joy, "Oh! I get to do this!"

If you are still seeking God for your assignment, begin by asking Him right now to show you and then to give you opportunities and occasions to serve Him. John Wesley, a great preacher and humble servant, lived by an incredible motto. Let his words motivate you to find God's assignment for your life and get to it. This is what he said:

Do all the good you can,
By all the means you can,
In all the ways you can,
In all the places you can,
At all the times you can,
To all the people you can,
As long as ever you can.[16]

You may need to start small, but start today. Remember, God is not looking for superstars. He is looking for servants. If you're not sure what that looks like, just take a long look at Jesus. Do what He did. Jesus will show you how to serve Him by loving others. Often, Jesus did small things in a great way. He served the sick. He cared for children. He cooked simple meals for His friends. He enjoyed great conversations. No assignment is too basic when you put your heart into it.

Sweet friend, remember that God created you and placed you on this earth for a purpose. It is with that purpose in mind that God has given you the means to accomplish it. Starting today, add Galatians 6:9 to your list of encouraging scriptures: "Let's not get tired of doing what is good. At just the right time we will reap a harvest of blessing if we don't give up" (NLT).

Read About His Love

Reread Colossians 3:23-24. As you do, think about Jochebed. She certainly didn't do what she did to receive the accolades of people. Rather, against human wisdom and likely her own emotions, she believed the word of the Lord and put her beautiful son in the Nile River.

Personalize the verse. I'll get you started:

*"Whatever **I** do, **I** will work at it with all **my** heart . . .*

Pray About His Love

It's a privilege to pray with you today. I know that God will use you either to do great things or to do small things in a great big way. Whatever you do for Him, do it with joy! Let me pray with you:

Dear loving Father,

I thank You that You have equipped me to serve You by serving others. My request today is that You would save the lost in the world around me. Comfort those who mourn. Raise up those who have fallen. Give shelter to those who are fighting the elements. Feed the hungry. Clothe the naked. Visit the sick and the prisoner. Love the unlovable and touch the untouchable. Lord, befriend those who are lonely. To accomplish these great tasks—use me to help You. I pray these things in Your precious name. Amen.

Be About His Love

Jesus told His disciples in Matthew 28:18-20 (NLT),

I have been given all authority in heaven and on earth. Therefore, go and make disciples of all the nations, baptizing them in the name of the Father and the Son and the Holy Spirit. Teach these new disciples to obey all the commands I have given you. And be sure of this: I am with you always, even to the end of the age.

Oh, yes, God's promise in you is incomparable. What part can you play today to help further His Great Commission? Remember, you're either a missionary or a mission project. Decide right now that you will be on mission and make a difference in the world for God. His assignment for you today may be as simple as letting someone who is in a hurry get ahead of you in traffic. It may mean committing to share your God-story before a small group. Whether your opportunity is a difficult task or something you could do with your eyes closed, commit this opportunity to the Lord and ask for His help to accomplish it with excellence.

DAY 5: ENVISION YOUR FUTURE

Those things, which ye have both learned, and received, and heard, and seen in me, do:
and the God of peace shall be with you.
Philippians 4:9 KJV

Think About His Love

> I consider everything a loss in comparison with the superior value of knowing Christ Jesus my Lord. (Philippians 3:8 CEB)

Your life is a reflection of who Christ is in you. Friends, embracing God's love for you will be a defining moment in your life if you allow it to be. You can get to the end of this study and say, "That was nice," and then pick up where you left off before you began. But instead, you could say, "That was then and this is now…and starting now, with the help of God, I will live like I know I'm God's favorite." From this moment forward, you can know and envision, beyond the shadow of any doubt, that

You are deeply loved by God, without condition.
You are complete in Him, lacking nothing.
You are never alone; God is with you.
Your needs are all met because God has supplied them.
You have a specific assignment to complete.
You are equipped with power to carry out that assignment.
Your God is faithful to complete the work He started in you.

In the third chapter of Philippians, Paul helps us hone in our life's goals by comparing who we once were to who we are now. He proclaims that his old life, even with his pedigree and personal accomplishments, paled in comparison to life in Christ. He said: "I consider everything a loss in comparison with the superior value of knowing Christ Jesus my Lord. I have lost everything for him, but what I lost I think of as sewer trash, so that I might gain Christ and be found in him" (Philippians 3:8-9a CEB).

In essence, Paul was reminding us that we can do all the right things for all the wrong reasons. We can hold onto our stuff and miss Christ and everything He has for us. We can be born into the right family, observe all the rules, be devoted to our church, and basically be good people. But apart from knowing Christ, all of that is worthless.

The Apostle Paul gave us permission to use his life as an example of what it really looks like to follow Christ without missing a beat. He told us to *stand firm,* another military term, meaning to stand our ground out on the battle front: not to be moved by popular opinion or shaken by what's going on around us but to stand firm according to Philippians 4:1: "Therefore, my brothers and sisters whom I love and miss, who are my joy and crown, stand firm in the Lord" (CEB).

Do you sense Paul's deep passion for us—members of the church body today—as he called his fellow Christ-followers "brothers and sisters…my joy and crown"? Paul wanted them, and I'm sure all who would come after them, to develop a similar passion for the body of Christ. I am certain he would want us to get this message today because if we don't get it—understanding that we all are part of something much bigger collectively than we are individually—we will succumb to the pressures of our culture and fail our mission.

Paul admitted that he was a work in progress—that we all are, for that matter—and he admonished us not to compromise our faith or lower our standards while we are on this road to becoming like Christ. So keep your eyes on the prize. In other words, keep your gaze fixed and your mind made up. Don't think like the world, act like the world, walk like the world, or talk like the world.

God wants you to stand on what you know to be true. Too often we are led by our feelings. A number of times throughout our study, I have reminded you to stand on what you know, not on what you feel. If the devil can control your feelings, then he can control how you live. So, make up your mind now that you will not be swayed by your emotions; instead, you will stand on what is reliable, trustworthy, faithful, genuine, and sure. When you stand on truth, you stand on the only thing that doesn't change, and that is the Word of God.

As you envision the life to which God has called you, remember that *He expects you to walk in unity with others*. We will never be effective for Christ as long as we are fussing and bickering, refusing to work together. Our enemy knows that we can do much more together than we can do apart. And if he can keep us divided, fighting among ourselves, then he doesn't have to lift a finger. We do the work of the enemy ourselves when we carelessly tear down a brother or sister in the Lord with our words and/or actions. *We must stand together, walk together, and work together.* By standing together in humility and thankfulness before God—acknowledging all our names appear together in His wonderful Book of Life—we can settle any confrontation with the power of God's love. In this earthly battle, we are complete in Christ as we stand together.

Years ago when I was a young piano student, I was instructed to practice thirty minutes a day. *The Baptist Hymnal* was my first piano method book. At the time, as a six-year-old, while my friends played kickball in the street, I was confined to the family den to practice my piano lessons. With my mother listening from the kitchen, I was assigned to practice those same hymns over and over again to the point of pure drudgery. A few decades later, all of that practice has proved to be quite beneficial.

In the same way, if we get into the habit of practicing all that we have learned concerning who and whose we are, we will grow together to become the church—the glorious, interdependent, and victorious spiritual body—that Father God has called us to be.

My mother, Mrs. Georgie Wade, is a great and godly woman. She's the mother of five brilliant children, of which I am the middle child. She served with my father, Pastor George W. Wade, as the founding first lady of the church where I grew up. On Mother's

Day weekend twenty-five years ago, Mom and I had the privilege of recording a mother-daughter interview for a radio station. Near the close of the interview, the host of the show asked my mom if she had some parting words. Mom is like E. F. Hutton. When she speaks, we lean in and listen. Mom said some words I will never forget. I'll leave these words with you now:

> People will often try to encourage you by telling you to "hang in there." But when people tell you to "hang in there," don't listen to them: because when you are hanging in there, you're vulnerable to your circumstances. You're exposed to the elements. You're at risk and susceptible to your weaknesses when you're hanging in there. The position of hanging paints the picture of dangling by a thread or by a noose. That's not the position you want to be in. You never want to hang in there! As believers, we are commanded to stand in there! As Ephesians 6 tells us: "Wherefore take unto you the whole armour of God, that ye may be able to withstand in the evil day, and having done all, to stand" (v. 13 KJV).

My mother said it best. Don't hang—stand! There is no need for you to hang in there because Jesus was already hung up for our hang-ups. He was stretched high and stretched wide, so we could stand strong on the truth of God's Word! No, dear friend, we don't need to hang in there. That is what Jesus did for us. He was hung up for each and every hang-up, habit, and hindrance.

Read About His Love

Years ago, I began writing a list of things I know to be true about God. Today, I am still adding to that list. It's quite a faith-building assignment, and I recommend you establish a list of your own.

For each of the Scriptures below, write I know statements that are truths about God. As you seek out these truths, begin to envision yourself living fully, unabashedly in the loving embrace of God.

John 1:1
I know . . .

1 John 4:7-8
I know . . .

Romans 8:28
I know . . .

Romans 8:31
I know . . .

Deuteronomy 7:9
I know . . .

1 John 4:4
I know . . .

Psalm 24:1
I know . . .

Ephesians 3:20
I know . . .

Romans 8:38-39
I know . . .

Matthew 27:50
I know . . .

Pray About His Love

Would you pray with me?

Dear heavenly Father,

You are amazing, God. Thank You for being right beside me as I discover Your embrace. Thank You for showing me how much You love me. Thank You for the gift of living life on purpose and for a purpose. What a gift that is! Help me to live my life according to Your plan. Let my life be a love song, a continual, sweet-smelling sacrifice of praise to You. In Jesus' name. Amen.

Be About His Love

As you envision your future as an embraced and loved child of God, what do you see? What purpose does your life fulfill? When you imagine doing the thing that God made you to do, what do you see? Sometimes in order to catch a glimpse of what God has for us we need to dream big. Write about what you see in the future as you cling to the embrace of God and live out His mission for your life. You might want to record your thoughts in the journaling pages in this book or in your own journal.

Week 7

VIDEO VIEWER GUIDE

Promise #7: You are equipped with unique _____ and _____.

In order to appreciate your gifts and talents and use them for God's glory, you must do three things:

    1. Encourage your _____.

    2. Equip your _____.

    3. Envision your _____.

Equipping yourself means this:

_____ God

_____ on God

_____ Godly Values

Whatever you do, work at it with all your heart, as working for _____ _____,

not for men, since you know that you will receive an inheritance from the Lord as a

reward. It is the Lord Christ you are _____.

                                                     Colossians 3:24 NIV

You can't be who you _____ to be without being who God _____ you to be.

Week 8

YOU CAN LIVE *LOVED*

I can't believe it, dear friend, but our time together has almost come to a close. After this week, we will close the chapter on this part of our spiritual journey and walk into the next one. Joining you at this place each day has been such a blessing to my soul. I believe the best is still yet to come for you. Long after we complete this *Embraced by God* encounter, I believe the blessings of God will continue to overtake you. God's promise from 1 Corinthians 2:9 (NKJV) comes to mind:

> *Eye has not seen, nor ear heard,*
> *Nor have entered into the heart of man*
> *The things which God has prepared for those who*
> *   love him.*

Remember that when times get tough (and you know that's the way life is), sometimes God will put your trouble out there "on the stage" for the whole world to see. But if you've rehearsed your lines, you'll know what to say when the spotlight is on you! This is your moment to shine, my dear friend. Make your Father proud.

And remember this: you can't be who you want to be without being the you God made you to be. On an ongoing basis, review your calling and constantly let God nudge you into the place you were meant to fit best. Make your Father's name famous in the earth.

The days ahead will present you with many opportunities to put what you've learned and experienced in this study into practice. This week will consider what it means to live *loved*—and that simply means living out the legacy of love you have inherited as a daughter of the Most High King. How? By fully returning God's amazing embrace. By standing firm on the promises of God. By being a blessing and shining a light everywhere you go. By confidently living out God's wonderful plan and purpose for your life. And by giving Him all the praise and glory for the wonderful life God has set before you. Get ready to live *loved,* sweet friend!

> You can't be who you want to be without being the you God made you to be.

Scripture Memorization

Throughout the week, continue focusing on our memory verse, John 17:23 (NCV):

"I will be in them and you will be in me so that they will be completely one. Then the world will know that you sent me and that you loved them just as much as you loved me."

Continue using the index cards in visible places and reading the verse when you get up, throughout the day, and as you go to bed. Remember that another great way to memorize Scripture is to write or type it.

DAY 1: KEEP SOWING IN LOVE

Summing up: Be agreeable, be sympathetic, be loving, be compassionate, be humble. That goes for all of you, no exceptions. No retaliation. No sharp-tongued sarcasm. Instead, bless—that's your job, to bless. You'll be a blessing and also get a blessing. Whoever wants to embrace life and see the day fill up good, Here's what you do: Say nothing evil or hurtful; Snub evil and cultivate good; run after peace for all you're worth.
1 Peter 3:8-11 *THE MESSAGE*

Think About His Love

Your love relationship with God is alive and active. In order for your love walk to grow to maturity, you must nurture it, tending to it every day. When I first started playing the piano for my father's church, full-time by age nine, I could only play in one key by ear—the key of C—since it was easier to navigate around the black keys on the piano. Although I was progressing as a young piano student, learning to play the compositions of Bach, Chopin, and Beethoven, that didn't help too much in church since no one in our choir could read music—and they weren't interested in a classical repertoire! Sometimes I hit a wrong note. Sometimes a song might have been too high. Sometimes a song might have been too low. And one time it was even too bad when I unknowingly played an entire song in a completely different key than that of the choir! But our entire church was so patient with me and encouraged me to develop my gifts and talents for God. They even paid me a nominal wage. The life lessons I learned in serving God and people were lessons that money could never buy. And as I continued practicing and playing with the choir, I cultivated my ability to play the piano.

Friends, as we enter our last week of readings and shared time together, I want to emphasize the importance of cultivating your love relationship with Jesus. To maximize your relationship with Him, you'll need to keep sowing to this vital relationship each day. The more "good seed" you sow, the more you'll grow. Just keep on giving. You will find that the more you give, the more God and people will give back to you. Our greatest joy in serving Christ comes by serving others. And as you refresh the lives of others, you will discover your own life being refreshed.

How does this work? First of all, remember that you're either a missionary or a mission project. The difference between the two is that missionaries know what it means to develop a lifestyle of giving. Just like a body of water grows stagnant if it has no outlet, the same is true of your life. Even if your efforts are small, little things will make a big difference. Missionaries understand this well.

I remember one day, I was on my way to speak to a group of women. While on the road I decided to drive through at a fast-food restaurant and grab a cup of coffee. As I was moving through the drive-thru, the Lord prompted me to buy lunch for the person in the car behind me. I didn't know who he or she was. I didn't know what the person had ordered. I just obeyed the Lord's prompting and told the clerk that I wanted to bless the person behind me by buying his or her lunch. I paid for it and drove off.

It's always interesting how things can work out when we obey God. Yes, I got blessed by this act of kindness, and I believe the person behind me was blessed. But I would also like to think the clerk working the drive-thru that day was affected as well. But that's not the end of the story.

The next day I was on my way back home again and went through another restaurant drive-thru to order a quick lunch. When I pulled up to the window to pay, I had misplaced my credit card and I didn't have any cash. The nice clerk at the window said, "Well, today, ma'am, your lunch is on the house!" He gave me my lunch for free! This is what you can expect when you sow into the lives of others.

It's easier now than ever before to share your love for Christ. Begin at home—in the house or apartment where you live, in your hometown, your home church, or your home school. Sharing from the heart of love is the nature of God's economy. No matter where you are, opportunities will always present themselves.

Christian singers often seek my counsel when desiring to jump-start their music ministries. They want suggestions on how to get started and get their ministry up on its legs. I always emphasize at "Inner Circle" gatherings for musicians that instead of waiting for a big break or spending a lot of money on promotion, simply find a place to serve. As long as there are hospitals, homes for drug rehabilitation, jails and prisons, and senior assisted living facilities, there will always be places to minister God's love. I encourage them to volunteer to visit one of these places on a Sunday afternoon. I suggest

> Our greatest joy in serving Christ comes by serving others. And as you refresh the lives of others, you will discover your own life being refreshed.

they tell some humorous stories to give folks a chance to enjoy some laughter, sing some fun songs that everybody knows, and conclude by telling their own God-story. Then I tell them to watch what happens. That doesn't mean they'll get paid monetarily, but I have found that one thing always leads to another. People who work in places like these are also involved in the community and in their church, and you never know when they'll call on willing volunteers to serve in another capacity.

This is good advice for all of us, regardless of our gifts. Sow. Give. This is the key— always be willing and ready to serve. Listen to what Jesus told Peter and the other disciples in Mark 11:22-24. His counsel still stands today:

> *Embrace this God-life. Really embrace it, and nothing will be too much for you. This mountain, for instance: Just say, "Go jump in the lake"—no shuffling or shilly-shallying—and it's as good as done. That's why I urge you to pray for absolutely everything, ranging from small to large. Include everything as you embrace this God-life, and you'll get God's everything. (THE MESSAGE)*

Read About His Love

Living *loved* means sowing in love. The principles of sowing and reaping apply to the love in our lives.

Read 2 Corinthians 9:6 and fill in the blanks below:

Whoever sows _____ will also

reap _____, and whoever

sows _____ will also reap

_____. (NIV)

Now read Galatians 6:7-8. What principle do we find in verse 7?

If we apply this principle to God's love, what conclusion can we draw?

Do not be deceived, God is not mocked; for whatever a man sows, that he will also reap. For he who sows to his flesh will of the flesh reap corruption, but he who sows to the Spirit will of the Spirit reap everlasting life. (Galatians 6:7-8 NKJV)

When we sow love, we reap love. The nature of God's love is to produce more and more love. When we sow in love, we come to live out of the overflow of the love of Jesus in our lives. His love fills us up and pours out into everyone we meet.

Make 1 Peter 3:8-11 from *THE MESSAGE* a personal prayer. Fill in the blanks to create your own prayer for living out this Scripture passage.

Be agreeable:
Lord, help me to

_____.

Be sympathetic:
Lord, help me to

_____.

Be loving:
Lord, help me to

_____.

Be compassionate:
Lord, help me to

_____.

Be humble:
Lord, help me to

_____.

No retaliation:
Lord, help me to

_____.

No sharp-tongued sarcasm:
Lord, help me to

_____.

Bless:
Lord, help me to

_____.

Embrace life:
Lord, help me to

_____.

Say nothing evil:
Lord, help me to

_____.

Say nothing hurtful:
Lord, help me to

_____.

Snub evil:
Lord, help me to

_____.

Cultivate good:
Lord, help me to

_____.

Run after peace:
Lord, help me to

_____.

Pray About His Love

Let's pray together that God would lead us to sow some love this week.

Dear heavenly Father,

You are awesome, amazing, almighty, and oh so wonderful. You have set before us a life of love and blessing. You have ordered our steps so that we will not fall. And when we think we'll go our own way for a while and end up with our face on the ground, You pick us up, dust us off, and wrap us up in Your loving embrace. You are just that good. So, Lord, fill us with Your love to overflowing. Help us to sow in love each and every day, planting seeds of love and kindness of hope and compassion. Nudge our hearts to do small things with great love. Set a great work before us and lead us with courage into Your purpose for us. We love You, Lord. In Jesus' name, I pray. Amen.

Be About His Love

Today, my friend, you have a mission. Your mission, if you choose to accept it, is to perform a random act of loving kindness to someone you meet along your way. Maybe you'll do what I did and pay for the car behind you in the drive-thru. Maybe you'll bake something special and take it to a friend. Maybe you'll send anonymous notes of gratitude to your children's teachers. Whatever you come up with, be intentional about sowing seeds of love and kindness. And then, just wait and watch; you will be blessed in your sowing.

DAY 2: KEEP GROWING IN LOVE

I am the vine; you are the branches. If a man remains in me and I in him, he will bear much fruit; apart from me you can do nothing.
John 15:5 NIV 1984

Think About His Love

Often, in times of quiet devotion, I will turn to one of the many church hymnals I've collected to read the lyrics of some of the church's great hymn writers. As I meditate upon the words that speak of their deep commitment to Christ, I prayerfully reflect upon my own Christian experience. With over eight thousand hymns and four books of poetry to her credit, Fannie Crosby is one of the most prolific composers the church has ever seen. Known as "The Queen of Gospel Song Writers," she wrote so many hymns that she used numerous pen names to conceal her identity. Even so, Fannie was widely known for her works and received recognition from governmental leaders and many civic organizations.

Blinded as a young toddler by a careless doctor's malpractice, Fanny grew to appreciate life in spite of what others considered a handicap. She wrote poetry as a child with such skill that her teachers marveled at her creativity. Maturing to be a great woman of faith, Fannie Crosby saw the beauty of life that few venture to experience.

Regardless of her personal circumstances, Fannie Crosby continued to express her deep trust and faith in the Lord through her music. She composed one of the most popular hymns the church has ever known, "Blessed Assurance." Each word sings of the believer's confidence in the Lord. In particular, the third stanza and chorus speak of the total reliance on which she based her love relationship with the Lord.

Perfect submission, all is at rest;
I in my Savior am happy and blessed,
watching and waiting, looking above,
filled with his goodness, lost in his love.

This is my story, this is my song,
praising my Savior all the day long;
this is my story, this is my song,
praising my Savior all the day long[17]

We can allow Fanny Crosby's life and music to serve as a beacon of hope for us, reminding us to keep growing in our faith and commitment to God. As long as there are life and breath in your body, you have the call from Christ to keep growing—to grow deeper, richer, and fuller in God's love.

Plain and simple, if you are not progressing in your spiritual walk, you are digressing—lagging behind, even growing stale and complacent. It's easy to just look the part, but don't be tempted to fake it until you make it in this regard. For example, visualize a silk flower or plant, or perhaps there is one within eyesight wherever you are right now. Silk plants are available in every color, shape, size, and texture, and they are becoming more and more popular these days. You can find them everywhere: in the mall, in airports, and in church. Silk plants are even being used in wreaths and floral arrangements for weddings and funerals.

But there's one element that silk plants just don't have. *Life.* They may look like the real thing, but if you move in for a closer look, if you touch a leaf or flower with your hand, or lean in to inhale its fragrance, you'll be sorely disappointed. You'll know immediately that it's an imposter. It's a fake, a phony.

While artificiality may work well for silk plants, there's no place for this characteristic in the life of the believer. Your spiritual life comes from staying connected to God and His Word. You know the value of meeting with God by now, so continue this spiritual discipline every day from now on. Keep going and you'll keep growing!

Before you can ever be effective in serving God publicly, you must practice His presence by serving Him privately. This is the mark of true maturity. Listen to these words from the Apostle Paul; they reflect his heartfelt desire to see every believer grow up in Christ:

No prolonged infancies among us, please. We'll not tolerate babes in the woods, small children who are an easy mark for imposters. God wants us to grow up, to know the whole truth and tell it in love—like Christ in everything. We take our lead from Christ, who is the source of everything we do. He keeps us in step with each other. His very breath and blood flow through us, nourishing us so that we will grow up healthy in God, robust in love.

Ephesians 4:14-16 *THE MESSAGE*

Maybe you have heard the old children's Bible school song, "He is the Vine and we are the branches..." That old familiar song is based on a beautiful passage from the Gospel of John, chapter 15. Jesus is teaching his disciples that in order to grow and produce fruit, we must stay connected to the Vine, which is our Father God. When we are connected to the life source, then we thrive and flourish with the fruit of our growth. If we become separated from the Vine, then our spiritual lives bear no fruit and wither up.

I don't know about you, but I do not like the image of withering up. I want to bear the fruit of my growth so that others can be blessed and come to know my God in a real and personal way.

It really all comes back to love. The message of unconditional love is God's absolute favorite message! You can journey through life unaffected by it, taking His love for granted, or you can walk and grow up into this unbelievable gift, allowing it to impact every area of your existence. The choice is yours. Remember what living *loved* is all about. Keep yourself constantly and consistently aware of God's loving presence in your life, knowing that God wishes to lavish His love on you with extreme generosity, abundance, and excessive liberality. Allow 1 John 3:1 to become a scriptural landmark in your life:

Before you can ever be effective in serving God publically, you must practice His presence by serving Him privately.

See what great love the Father has lavished on us, that we should be called children of God. (NIV)

In a world where far too many people have forgotten about God, and even more have forgotten that He loves them, determine to be one of those who will rise high above the crowd and shout from the mountaintop: *There is a great big God, and His love is available for the whole wide world!*

So, the next time you hear the words *God loves you,* I hope you ponder for just a little while the great price that was paid for you to be embraced by God. May this awesome promise reduce you to a humble heap of eternal gratitude. That's exactly what happens to me when I pause and consider God's love.

Dear friend, I pray you come to understand this powerful truth in an ever-increasing way. Just think about it. Of the seven billion people on the face of the planet, God loves you as if you were the only one to love. May this truth forever rock your world! And as you grow up into this truth each and every day, returning the Father's embrace, may you grow and bear much fruit, and never, ever be the same.

Read About His Love

To grow in our love relationship with Jesus, we have to stay connected to Him.

Take a look at Ephesians 4:14-16 again. Underline phrases that are instructions for growing in love.

> *No prolonged infancies among us, please. We'll not tolerate babes in the woods, small children who are an easy mark for imposters. God wants us to grow up, to know the whole truth and tell it in love—like Christ in everything. We take our lead from Christ, who is the source of everything we do. He keeps us in step with each other. His very breath and blood flow through us, nourishing us so that we will grow up healthy in God, robust in love.*
>
> **Ephesians 4:14-16 *THE MESSAGE***

Read John 15. In the space below, draw a vine and some branches. Write "Jesus" on the vine. Then, on the branches, write some words that describe some of the fruit that comes from a committed life with Jesus.

Now, write a few words about what John 15 says about growing in love. As you have time, use these thoughts as a springboard for writing a journal entry about what you can do to grow in love.

Pray About His Love

Let's pray together as we commit ourselves completely to Christ, making ourselves available to receive this love that is beyond all comprehension, and then to bear much fruit as we grow in this love.

Dear heavenly Father,

We thank You that You know exactly what we need in order to grow and thrive for You. You bless us with every good thing. Lord, forgive us for the times that we have willingly and knowingly turned away from You. Cut off every branch in us that holds sin and ugliness. Cut off every branch that thinks we are better off left to our own opinions and ways. God, only Your ways are truly perfect. Only Your ways are good. Give us the courage, wisdom, and guidance to walk in Your good and perfect way. And most of all, Loving God, help us grow in love and to seek You with all our hearts. God, we give ourselves to the journey of being held in Your warm, loving, and gentle embrace. In Jesus' name, I pray. Amen.

Be About His Love

Today, I want you to go outside and observe the trees and flowers in your area. Look for signs of life and also note any branches that are not producing any growth. If it is winter and there is no growth, give special attention to the barrenness of your surroundings. Sit with your journal and take an assessment of the fruit that your spiritual life currently bears. What areas of your life feel cut off from the vine and stagnant or even dead? Friends, let's invite God to cut off those dead branches and free us to grow and produce beautiful fruit.

DAY 3: KEEP WALKING IN LOVE

Who shall separate us from the love of Christ? Shall trouble or hardship or persecution or famine or nakedness or danger or sword?
Romans 8:35

Think About His Love

I don't claim to be an athlete by any means, but one year I participated in a Labor Day 10K road race. For weeks I trained. (As a matter of fact, one of my former middle school students who is now an experienced marathon runner was my coach.) I'll never forget training for that race. I'm not a runner, but I committed to walking the 6.2-mile hike. The course was a tough one. Sometimes I wondered what possessed me to try such a thing. Some people passed me by, but I'd come too far to turn back, so I just kept putting one foot in front of the other. Sometimes we walked up long, steeply graded hills. Then we had to come down the other side of those steep hills, each arduous step placing us closer to the finish line. When we reached the goal, crowds of people where there to celebrate our victory with us. I got a T-shirt and my own personal medal from my coach, but the real reward was the reality of this great accomplishment in my own life.

So allow me to cheer you on. I'm sure you know this by now, sweet friend, but just in case you need a reminder: you will be tired from taking life's hills. You're going to get disappointed, or discouraged; some days you'll just have to determine to keep on walking.

It's on days like these that you'll just need to keep going. Just keep walking. Keep putting one foot in front of the other and keep moving forward. Keep walking in the love that God has for you.

See yourself as God sees you—loved beyond your capacity to imagine, saved from your sin, and free to live the life He has planned for you. When you really take hold of this life-changing truth, it will impact the way you think and ultimately the way you live.

Keep reminding yourself over and over again that you are loved by God. It's great that you love God. This is the first commandment God gives us. But once you lay hold of how much God loves you, you will grasp a life-changing truth. I love the fact that John, the author of the book that bears his name, considered himself to be the disciple whom Jesus loved! John knew something that we must know deep down inside, something that we must celebrate each and every day. *He knew that to love God was one thing, but to be loved by God, to be considered God's favorite, changes your life forever.*

Dear one, don't let anything come between you and God's love for you. Don't let guilt separate you. Don't let shame separate you. Don't let your past mistakes separate you. Nothing, beloved friend! Don't let anything separate you from God's love. Listen to the Apostle Paul's victorious statement. I encourage you to memorize this powerful passage:

> *Do you think anyone is going to be able to drive a wedge between us and Christ's love for us? There is no way! Not trouble, not hard times, not hatred, not hunger, not homelessness, not bullying threats, not backstabbing, not even the worse sins listed in Scripture.... None of this fazes us because Jesus loves*

> To love God [is] one thing, but to be loved by God, to be considered God's favorite, changes your life forever.

us. I'm absolutely convinced that nothing—nothing living or dead, angelic or demonic, today or tomorrow, high or low, thinkable or unthinkable—absolutely nothing can get between us and God's love because of the way that Jesus our Master has embraced us.

Romans 8:35, 37-39 *THE MESSAGE*

I am reminded again of my dad, Pastor George Wade. He was a great preacher, pastor, prison chaplain, college professor, and public servant. Like the Apostle Paul said of himself, Dad was all things to all people that he might win some (see 1 Corinthians 9:22 NKJV). He and my mother, Mrs. Georgie Wade, were married almost fifty years and served diligently together in one church for nearly forty years. I learned how to serve God and the church by observing their tireless example.

Dad passed away twenty-five years ago. He left a great legacy: an insatiable appetite for the things of God, an enviable passion for His Word, and an undying love for His church. Long after his death, Dad still encourages me to do great things for God and for people.

It is from his example that I want to inspire you. Dad died on March 4, 1987. Even today his victorious "home going" challenges us to march forth—to never give in to the pressure from the world around us, but to march forth and press on in the gospel. Keep putting one foot in front of the other with diligence, determination, and love.

You see, my friend, God will use you to make an eternal difference if you make yourself available to Him. You may feel like saying, "Well, I'm just an ordinary person. I'm nobody special. God couldn't possibly use me." And apart from Christ, you'd be absolutely correct in saying that. The Bible says that you can do nothing without Him. But you are in Christ! And as you yield yourself to Him, placing your life in His loving, capable hands, you find yourself being the perfect candidate to be used by God to do extraordinary things. Remember, you are God's favorite. He loves you as much as He loves Jesus.

God is looking for someone just like you to spread His love in all the earth!

Read About His Love

Just as my dad gave me an insatiable appetite for the things of God, no doubt you have your own encouragers in your life who call you to press on in faith. I'm so glad that God provides these "witnesses" in our lives who spur us on to be women who love God and who want to be used by Him to make a difference in this world.

Read Hebrews 12:1-3 and answer the following questions.

Who are the individuals that make up your "cloud of witnesses"—those who are still living in this world and those who have passed on to be with Jesus?

What do these verses instruct us to do?

Throw off _____

Run with _____

Fix our eyes on _____

When you reflect on Jesus and all that he endured—in life and in death—what thoughts come to mind?

How can thinking about Jesus help you to persevere and not lose heart?

When you have down days or when you doubt your ability to do any good for God—as we all occasionally do—remember these Bible truths and walk boldly in love.

Read Romans 7:15-25 and answer the following questions.

When have you felt the spiritual battle within you as Paul did when he said, "What I want to do I do not do, but what I hate I do" (v. 15 NIV)?

When we have bad days and make bad choices, what encouragement can we find in these words of Paul? (vv. 24-25)

Now, read Romans 8:35, 37-39. Write these verses in your own words below and claim this promise today and every time you have trouble walking in love.

Read 1 Corinthians 9:19-27. What does this passage from Paul tell you about being committed to a love relationship with Jesus Christ?

Pray About His Love

Today I'd like to pray with you by using these words I wrote just for today. I'll encourage you to make these words your own.

Sweet Father in heaven,
Let me walk each day with You
Embracing every step
Let me feel Your hand in mine
You've never failed me yet

The hills are steep and hard to climb
The valleys dark and low
So I'll not trust in how I feel
But trust the One I know

I don't understand this kind of love
So lavish, rich and true
But from the bottom of my heart
I'm grateful that You do
In Jesus' wonderful name I pray. Amen.

Be About His Love

To practice walking in love each and every day, I want to give you a challenge. Starting tomorrow morning, when you get up out of your bed, start your day by saying this:

God, I don't deserve it, but thank You for loving me the way You do. Help me to love You with all my heart. Then give me the power and the desire to love everyone I come in contact with today with this kind of love!

DAY 4: KEEP BONDED IN SISTERHOOD

So let's do it—full of belief, confident that we're presentable inside and out. Let's keep a firm grip on the promises that keep us going. He always keeps his word. Let's see how inventive we can be in encouraging love and helping out, not avoiding worshiping together as some do but spurring each other on, especially as we see the big Day approaching.
Hebrews 10:25 *THE MESSAGE*

Think About His Love

Throughout this study I have shared with you the love and admiration I have for my father. I hope you are able to conclude just how much my dad meant to me. Because he was the pastor and I was the pianist, we spent a lot of time together. We'd ride to and from church together and plan the worship services. It was a distinct joy to play the piano for Dad when he'd sing a song before he preached his sermons. Even when Dad would be invited to another city to preach, I'd be right there to play the piano and sing. Because we spent those precious times together, I consider myself Dad's favorite.

But I have a younger sister, Benita. If you were to ask her, you'd get an entirely different perspective. Growing up, Benita was a bit of a tomboy. Our family loves sports, and all my brothers played baseball, football, and basketball. We attended all of their sporting events and played ball together with all the neighborhood kids. So Dad and Benita spent lots time playing ball in the driveway. He'd show Benita how to slide into second base and how to choke up on the baseball bat. She also demonstrated great administrative skills, even as a kid. So Dad put Benita to work typing the Sunday morning worship bulletin and helping out in the church office.

So if you ask her, she'd tell you that she was Dad's favorite. As a matter of fact, I did ask her as I was preparing for this study, and that was her exact response! I've figured it out now. Dad assured all of us that we were his favorite. This speaks to the kind of father we had—one who made each of us feel special, chosen, and preferred.

This is the way it is with our relationship with the Lord. Each of us is loved as if we were the only one to love. Knowing that He loves you like this doesn't take a single thing away from me. Not for a moment! On the contrary, it adds joy to my life knowing that our Father loves us like this. The bond between us as sisters is that much stronger and sweeter. Because of this, I want to see you grow stronger in your faith. That's why I can meet you for the first time and almost feel like I know you. I already know in my heart that you are experiencing joy and heartache, victories and defeats, laughter and tears— just like me. We may come from different parts of the country or even the world. We may have different accents when we speak or even be a different race, but this is what makes the body of Christ beautiful. This common bond of love and faith in Christ is what makes us family.

We can receive help for keeping bonded in sisterhood from the Apostle Paul's words about two women who started out working together but somewhere along the line had a disagreement and ended up being at odds with each other. We read about them in Philippians 4:2-3 (NIV):

> *I plead with Euodia and I plead with Syntyche to agree with each other in the Lord. Yes, and I ask you, loyal yokefellow, to help these women who have contended at my side in the cause of the gospel, along with Clement and the rest of my fellow workers, whose names are in the book of life.*

The relationship with these two women was apparently adversarial and strained. So much so that the Apostle Paul assigned a "loyal yokefellow" to help these women get along. Their disagreement was so volatile, in fact, that these two women, who were obviously well respected, were in danger of affecting the entire church. May this never be said of us, my dear sister. Instead, may we be known as women who make the cause of Christ our only agenda.

Let's agree that promoting the gospel of Jesus is what we will always be about. When we come together to worship, our focus and our aim must be only to lift up the name of Jesus Christ. Reaching the lost, the hurting, and the next generation is our priority. Listen to these words from Hebrews 10:24-25 (NIV):

> *And let us consider how we may spur one another on toward love and good deeds. Let us not give up meeting together, as some are in the habit of doing, but let us encourage one another—and all the more as you see the Day approaching.*

Read About His Love

Let us be reminded never to compromise our love for God or our love for a sister in the Lord. We must do all we can to encourage her and add to her life. The possibility is great that she is need of an encouraging word or deed. Of course, we won't agree on everything, but when we don't see eye to eye on a particular matter, let's agree that we will love one another and resolve the matter for the good of all. This is what Christ would have us to do. Let's hold each other accountable in this area.

Read the following passages and write the message of encouragement or instruction found in each:

Philippians 4:2-3

Let us not become weary in doing good, for at the proper time we will reap a harvest if we do not give up. (Galatians 6:9 NIV)

Philippians 4:8-9

Galatians 6:9

Reread Philippians 4:2-3. How would you advise Euodia and Syntyche to resolve their differences?

How do you imagine that their relationship got to this volatile stage?

Read 1 Thessalonians 5:11. Why is it important to build each other up with words of encouragement?

How can your words make a difference in your relationships with friends and family?

Pray About His Love

Let's pray for our relationships with our sisters in the Lord.

Dear heavenly Father,

Thank You for the strong, godly women you have placed in our lives. Help us to build each other up and never to tear each other down. When our words and actions hurt or wound another sister, may we seek forgiveness and reconciliation immediately. Help us to remember to add blessings to the lives of those we love, always being ready to deliver kind words and deeds. And when we disagree, help us to understand that it's okay to disagree. Then guide us in resolving each disagreement with love, keeping in mind what is best for everyone involved. Forgive us when we are selfish. Give us a heart like Yours. I need my sisters and only want to bless them. Help me to show them how much they mean to me. In the name of Jesus I pray. Amen.

Be About His Love

As you go about living *loved* today, remember this powerful thought: We are all family. We don't have the same mother, but we have the same Father—our heavenly Father. He looks at each of us as His favored one. Carry this thought with you and share it with someone today. In the Old Testament, the inhabitants of Moab were called Moabites, the people who occupied the land of Canaan were known as Canaanites, and the people of Israel were known as Israelites. Because we occupy the land of God's favor, we are known as Favor-ites. Remind someone today that she or he is God's favorite.

DAY 5: KEEP GIVING YOUR LIFE TO CHRIST

"For God so loved the world that he gave his one and only Son, that whoever believes in him shall not perish but have eternal life."
John 3:16 NIV

Think About His Love

What a journey we have been on these last eight weeks! It has been my privilege and joy to walk with you through this experience of being embraced by God. When you make the decision to receive God's embrace and walk in His love each day, returning that embrace, your life will never be the same. So many incredible and unforgettable new experiences are ahead of you in your love embrace with the Lord.

During the video for Week 3, I extended an invitation for you to accept God's loving embrace and receive the gifts of forgiveness and friendship made possible by Jesus' death on the cross—whether for the first time or as an act of renewing your relationship with Him. When you make this vitally important decision to receive and embrace God's love, your life is never the same.

To live *loved,* you must keep your love relationship with the Lord vibrant and strong, and this involves continually giving your life to Christ. One of the best ways to do this is always to be mindful of God's precious gift of salvation—what it is and what it means. Regularly revisiting these truths from the Bible will keep your commitment strong as you are filled to overflowing with humility, gratitude, and praise:

The Reality. God loves you and wants to have a personal relationship with you! Revelation 3:20 says, "Behold, I stand at the door and knock. If anyone hears My voice and opens the door, I will come in to him and dine with him, and he with Me" (NKJV).

The Problem. Because of sin, everyone in the world has been born spiritually dead. Romans 6:23 says, "For the wages of sin is death; but the gift of God is eternal life, through Jesus Christ our Lord."

The Promise. Jesus will forgive us of every sin, promising us eternal life with Him in eternity! First John 1:9 tells us, "If we confess our sins, he is faithful and just to forgive us our sins, and to cleanse us from all unrighteousness." Added to this, Jesus promised in John 14:1-3 (NIV),

> *Do not let your hearts be troubled. Trust in God; trust also in me. In my Father's house are many rooms; if it were not so, I would have told you. I am going there to prepare a place for you. And if I go and prepare a place for you, I will come back and take you to be with me that you also may be where I am.*

The Plan. God's gift of salvation is exactly that: a *gift*. To receive it, we simply confess that we are sinners and invite Jesus to come into our lives and forgive us of our sins. Jesus was crucified, died, and rose again for this very reason. It is accomplished. All the work has been done. There is nothing we must do. All that is necessary is to receive the gift. And once we do, from that moment forward God never stops working to help us become all He designed us to be.

With these truths fresh on our minds as we end our time together, it seems fitting for us to make a declaration of commitment. You might be a new believer, or you might be an on-again, off-again disciple who wants to make a determined choice to love and serve Jesus with your whole heart from this point forward. Or perhaps you are a long-time follower who wants to renew your love walk with the Lord. Wherever you are in your journey, let's close our time together by joining in a commitment to walk in our identity as daughters of the Most High King, following Jesus with *all* of our hearts.

I've written a statement called The Declaration that expresses this commitment and calls to mind important declarations about who we are in Christ. You will revisit this declaration with your sisters in your final group session this week, and you will be given the opportunity to recite it together as a public profession of your ongoing commitment. For now, I'd like you to spend a few minutes meditating on these words privately. Make this a sweet time of declaring your love and commitment to the Lord.

The Declaration
I Am a Daughter of the Most High King

I am a daughter of the Most High King. I am deeply loved, highly favored, and greatly blessed. My identity is in Christ alone. I know who I am and Whose I am. I am the righteousness of God in Christ. I am accepted in the Beloved and a joint heir together with Him. I am a part of the Family of God and the Holy Spirit dwells in me.

I will follow Jesus with all my heart. There will be no turning around, no slacking up, no backing down, no striking out, and no giving in. I will not compromise my faith, lower my standards, or cower in the face of adversity. My past is forgiven. My present has purpose, and my best and brightest days are still ahead of me. I walk by faith and not by sight. My gaze is fixed and my mind is made up. I am determined not to think like the world, walk like the world, talk like the world, or act like the world. I shall not be moved. I cannot be shaken. And I will not be swayed. I belong to Jesus and I set my sights on things above. Earth is my mission and Heaven is my destiny.

I confess that I can do all things through Christ Who strengthens me. All things are possible. So if God is for me, who can be against me? My faith is rooted and established in love, and nothing I have done or ever will do can ever diminish the height, the depth, the length, and the breadth of God's love for me. I am convinced that neither death, nor life, angels or demons, the present, the future, or any powers will be able to separate me from the love of God, which is in Christ Jesus our Lord.

I eagerly await Christ's return. And on that great day He will know me and call me by name. His banner over me is love and I will lift my voice in loudest hallelujahs to sing His praises forevermore. For I am a daughter of the Most High King!

Read About His Love

I just love stories of salvation in Jesus Christ. Let's look at two we find in the New Testament.

Read Luke 19:1-10. Who are the main characters in this story?

What did Jesus say to the man?

How was the man saved?

Read Acts 16:16-34. Who are the main characters in this story?

What happened to Paul and Silas?

What amazing thing happened?

How did the people respond?

Like Zacchaeus and the jailer and his family, you have learned to accept God's embrace on your life, and you have chosen to return that sweet embrace. Now let's make sure we know how to share God's loving embrace with others. When you ponder how you would share the story of salvation with others, you might wonder what to say. I want us to look at Paul's teaching about salvation in Ephesians 2:1-10 for some guidance.

Read Ephesians 2:1-10 and answer the following questions.

What condition were we in before our life in Christ?

What does verse 4 say about God?

What did God do for us?

How are we saved?

For what are we saved?

Pray About His Love

I am so excited to pray for you today—the final day of our time together before we gather for the last group session. Be assured, my friend, that everyone who reads this book and participates in this study will continually be in my prayers. I will be lifting you up repeatedly! Oh sweet friend, may you never forget how precious you are to Jesus and to me. Keep at the forefront of your mind that you are God's favorite and that He loves you just as much as He loves Jesus. May you always know the height, depth, length, and breadth of His love for you. Let me pray with you once more.

Dear loving, awesome, amazing Father,

To know that we are loved intimately by the Creator of the whole universe is just too wonderful to take in. These last eight weeks have been an amazing journey. To know without any doubt that You love us as much as You love Jesus, that we are Your favorite, is a wonderful revelation! And now this love revelation has sparked a love revolution!

Out of the overflow of Your love for us we can love others. So we pray for our sisters who are in desperate need. Only Your loving hand and warm embrace can com-

fort and heal them where they hurt the most. But we give You permission to use us as living examples to show them Your love.

So many women have never known Your love before. Draw them by Your Spirit and keep them grounded in Your Word. And for my sisters who are thriving now—keep them tapped into the Vine. May they always know the rich and satisfying life.

God, as we close this chapter and walk into Your purpose for us, help us to live loved, always being constantly and consciously aware of Your loving presence in our lives. We promise to walk with You, confident of the work You began in us here. In Jesus' sweet and precious name, I pray. Amen.

Be About His Love

You have been on an incredible journey of falling into God's embrace and learning to walk with purpose into His amazing future for you. I couldn't end a journey like this without imploring you to share it with others. Jesus calls us to take His gospel into all the world. Friends, as you grow more and more in love with Jesus, I ask you to covenant right now to share His love, His story, His healing, His teaching, and His grace with everyone with whom you come in contact.

Listen for the Holy Spirit's leading and be open to that holy nudge when you are led to share about or act for Jesus. Keep a list in your journal of every time you get a call or a leading from the Holy Spirit and act on it. Go back and add notes when you see that God has used you to bring someone else to Him or to do an exciting work in His name.

There will be people who will forget how much they are loved by a great, big God. Please, my sister, don't be one of them. May you always be mindful of God's great, relentless, fiery love for you. May this eternal truth forever rock your world. As you walk out this Embraced by God life, returning the Father's love, may you never be the same.

VIDEO VIEWER GUIDE

Three things you can do to live *loved:*

1. _____ in love.

"_____ *this God-life. Really embrace it, and nothing will be*

too much for you. This mountain, for instance: Just say, 'Go jump in the lake'—

no shuffling or shilly-shallying—and it's as good as done. That's why I urge you

to _____ for absolutely _____, ranging from

small to large. Include everything as you embrace this God-life, and you'll get

God's everything."

Mark 11:22-24 *THE MESSAGE*

2. _____ in love.

3. _____ in love.

NOTES

1. Eyewitness to History.com, "Henry Ford Changes the World, 1908," http://www.eyewitnessto history.com/ford.htm, accessed June 2, 2012.

2. Mario Andretti, http://www.biography.com/people/mario-andretti-9184819.

3. Johann Sebastian Bach, "Soli Deo gloria," www.Christianity.com/churchhistory/11635057.

4. Tony Evans, *Tony Evans' Book of Illustrations* (Chicago: Moody, 2009), 172–73.

5. Andrew Stanley, North Point TV with Andy Stanley, North Point Community Church, 4350 North Point Parkway, Alpharetta, GA 30022, www.northpoint.org.

6. Based on Martin Luther, "Out of the Depths," www.hymnary.org/hymn/UMH/515.

7. John 21:15-17, *agape* (25, GK.); *thelo* (2309, GK); *phileo* (5368, GK), in *Strongs Talking Greek and Hebrew Dictionary* (Austin: WORDsearch, 2005).

8. J. D. Douglas II and Norman Hillyer, *eros* in T*yndale New Bible Dictionary,* 2nd ed. (Leicester, England: Universities and Colleges Christian Fellowship, 1982), 711.

9. *Agape,* in Douglas and Hillyer, *Tyndale.*

10. Barbara Crossett, "Foreign Aid Budget: Quick, How Much? Wrong," www.nytimes.com/1995/02/27/world/foreign-aid-budget-quick-how-much-wrong.html.

11. *Phileo se,* in Douglas and Hillyer, *Tyndale New Bible Dictionary.*

12. Sydney Smith, http://en.thinkexist.com/quotes/Sydney_Smith/.

13. "Depression," accessed November 17, 2011, www.emedicinehealth.com/depression/article_em.htm.

14. Willa Ward-Royster, *How I Got Over: Clara Ward and the World Famous Ward Singers* (Philadelphia: Temple UP, 1997), x, 99, 104, 237. "How I Got Over," Admin. By ASCAP.

15. Exodus 6:20, *Jochebed* (3115, Heb) in *Strong's Talking Greek and Hebrew Dictionary* (Austin: WORDsearch, 2005).

16. This quote has been attributed to John Wesley, although some historians have noted that there is no evidence showing he actually wrote it. See Mary Jacobs, "Wesley, Misquoted," in *The United Methodist Reporter,* http://umportal.org/article.asp?id=8201, accessed June 1, 2012.

17. Fannie Crosby, "Blessed Assurance," 1873 (*The United Methodist Hymnal,* The United Methodist Publishing House, 1989), 369.

Journaling

Journaling